*Black Winning Jockeys
in the Kentucky Derby*

ALSO BY JAMES ROBERT SAUNDERS
AND FROM MCFARLAND

*Tightrope Walk: Identity, Survival and the Corporate World
in African American Literature* (1997)

*The Wayward Preacher in the Literature
of African American Women* (1995)

BY JAMES ROBERT SAUNDERS
AND RENAE NADINE SHACKELFORD
AND FROM MCFARLAND

*The Dorothy West Martha's Vineyard: Stories,
Essays and Reminiscences by Dorothy West
Writing in the* Vineyard Gazette (2001)

*Urban Renewal and the End of Black Culture
in Charlottesville, Virginia: An Oral History
of Vinegar Hill* (1998)

Black Winning Jockeys in the Kentucky Derby

JAMES ROBERT SAUNDERS
and
MONICA RENAE SAUNDERS

McFarland & Company, Inc., Publishers
Jefferson, North Carolina, and London

Library of Congress Cataloguing-in-Publication Data

Saunders, James Robert, 1953–
    Black winning jockeys in the Kentucky Derby / James Robert Saunders and Monica Renae Saunders.
        p.   cm.
    Includes bibliographical references and index.

    ISBN 0-7864-1402-2 (softcover : 60# alkaline paper) ∞

    1. African American jockeys—Biography. 2. African American jockeys—History. 3. Horse racing—Kentucky—History. 4. Kentucky Derby, Louisville, Ky.—History. I. Saunders, Monica Renae. II. Title.
    SF336.A2S28   2003
    798.4'0092'396073—dc21   2002013886

British Library cataloguing data are available

©2003 James Robert Saunders and Monica Renae Saunders. All rights reserved

No part of this book may be reproduced or transmitted in any form or by any means, electronic or mechanical, including photocopying or recording, or by any information storage and retrieval system, without permission in writing from the publisher.

Manufactured in the United States of America

Cover photograph: Alonzo "Lonnie" Clayton *(Keeneland Library, Lexington, KY)*

McFarland & Company, Inc., Publishers
  Box 611, Jefferson, North Carolina 28640
  www.mcfarlandpub.com

For the ones who have faded
beyond the pale of history

ACKNOWLEDGMENTS

This project was conceived in 1996, when we visited the Kentucky Derby Museum and happened upon an extraordinary display marking the contributions that blacks had made to the Derby, most notably the contributions of certain black jockeys and trainers. It was an enlightening experience, but even more, it was a haunting experience, for we had suddenly been exposed to the reality of a profound and substantial contribution that had all but disappeared from the larger public view. A lifesize cardboard cut-out of the jockey Isaac Murphy seemed to beckon us to delve more deeply into the past, to discover more about who he in particular was, beckoned us to discover more about the others who were in some ways just like him. Needless to say, we were mesmerized, powerless to ignore that jockey's piercing eyes glimmering with pride but also tearful, as we perceived it, that history had not been kind to him and his compatriots.

After that visit to the Downs, our job became clear as we set ourselves to the task of uncovering as much information as we could about the African American jockeys who had won the Kentucky Derby. We are grateful to Diedre L. Badejo, a professor at the University of Louisville, for her part in creating the museum display. It had been our aim just to take in Churchill Downs on our visit to the city. But once we got there, that display made the trip more meaningful than we ever could have imagined.

Jay Ferguson, director of Curatorial Services at the Kentucky Derby Museum, also provided valuable assistance, as did Tony Terry, director of the Publicity Department at Churchill Downs, who not only arranged for our use of certain photographs, but was also kind enough to forward us the Kentucky Derby guidebook for 1998, an especially important issue for our particular purposes. Also helpful in the acquisition of photographs was Ann S. Tatum, curator of Kentucky Derby Photo Files at the Kinetic Corporation. Phyllis Rogers, at the Keeneland Library in Lexington, Kentucky, was a key source of encouragement, in addition to providing photographs that she had reproduced for their inclusion in this book.

Steve Rizzo, at Berry's Camera Shop in Lafayette, Indiana, was always available for our various photographic needs. We are grateful for the countless times that he pulled himself away from some other project with which he was involved so that he could give us his assistance. It just so happens that as we were finishing this book, he was also finishing his work at Berry's and has since moved on to Madison, Indiana, to assume proprietorship of his own photography studio. It was, to say the least, quite fortuitous that we happened to be in the same place at the same time when we were in need of his talents.

Over the course of this four-year project, the authors were affiliated with five educational institutions. The Greenhills School in Ann Arbor, Michigan, served as an important resource center. At the University of Michigan, in that same city, the Interlibrary Loans Department was essential as well as the Serials and Microforms Department, notably in the person of Demetra Demarakos, whose efforts went beyond the call of duty.

Our move to West Lafayette, Indiana, and Purdue University in particular, was fortuitous beyond just the fact that it put us in close vicinity to Rizzo. At the Storage Facility of Purdue's John W. Hicks Library, we were able to locate the original issues of key periodicals, some of which were a century old and in excellent condition. We took full advantage of that resource as well as the opportunity to work under the auspices of a Purdue course, entitled "Black Jockeys," which gave us further time to organize our ideas and materials.

Finally, we must thank the early Kentucky Derby jockeys themselves, those who were at one time heralded as well as those who went virtually unnoticed. The Epsom Derby in rural England may have served as the inspiration for M. Lewis Clark to return to Louisville and begin a racetrack at Churchill Downs. And the early owners were certainly an important key for the development of the Kentucky Derby into its current prominence. Trainers were likewise essential. But it was the jockeys and their gifted horses who, in the Derby's early years, cut a swath so wide across the turf that in retrospect it is utterly amazing.

Table of Contents

Acknowledgments — vii
List of Illustrations — xi
Introduction — 1

I:	Oliver Lewis—May 17, 1875	9
II:	William Walker—May 22, 1877	19
III:	James Carter—May 21, 1878	25
IV:	George Garrett Lewis—May 18, 1880	28
V:	"Babe" Hurd—May 16, 1882	33
VI:	Erskine "Babe" Henderson—May 14, 1885	38
VII:	Isaac Lewis—May 11, 1887	44
VIII:	Isaac Murphy—May 16, 1884; May 14, 1890; May 13, 1891	50
IX:	Alonzo Clayton—May 11, 1892	66
X:	James Perkins—May 6, 1895	72
XI:	Willie Simms—May 6, 1896; May 4, 1898	77
XII:	James Winkfield—April 29, 1901; May 3, 1902	87

Conclusion — 97

Appendix A: Summary of Black Kentucky Derby Winners	111
Appendix B: Black Owners of Kentucky Derby Horses	112
Appendix C: Black Trainers of Kentucky Derby Horses	113
Notes	115
Bibliography	121
Index	125

LIST OF ILLUSTRATIONS

Black lawn jockey (photograph by Monica Saunders).	2
Black stable hands relaxing between working hours (*Outing*, 1902).	5
Churchill Downs in 1903 (courtesy of the Keeneland Library).	7
Charles E. Van Loan's short story characters Moseby Jones and Old Man Curry plotting strategy (drawing by F. C. Yohn for *Collier's*, 1915).	10
McGrathiana, home of H. Price McGrath, who owned Aristides, winner of the first Kentucky Derby in 1875 (*Outing*, 1900).	12
Exercise boy, a job once held primarily by blacks (*Outing*, 1908).	13
Oliver Lewis (courtesy of the Keeneland Library).	15
William Walker (courtesy of Churchill Downs, Inc./Kinetic Corp.).	20
Brown, trainer of 1877 Kentucky Derby winner Baden-Baden (courtesy of the Keeneland Library).	22
Ashland, the farm where John M. Clay bred 1878 Kentucky Derby winner Day Star (*Outing*, 1900).	27
Isaac Lewis (courtesy of Churchill Downs, Inc./Kinetic Corp.).	46

List of Illustrations

Milton Young, breeder of 1887 Kentucky Derby winner Montrose (*Outing*, 1900).	47
Isaac Murphy (courtesy of the Keeneland Library).	52
Isaac Murphy and associates at a clambake (courtesy of the Keeneland Library).	62
Charles E. Van Loan's fictional Moseby Jones hoisted in celebration after a victory (drawing by F. C. Yohn for *Collier's*, 1916).	63
Alonzo Clayton (courtesy of the Keeneland Library).	67
James "Soup" Perkins (courtesy of the Keeneland Library).	73
Willie Simms (*Munsey's Magazine*, 1900).	79
James Winkfield (courtesy of the Keeneland Library).	88
Jimmy Lee (courtesy of the Keeneland Library).	100
Jockey fouled early in the twentieth century in an effort to deter him and other blacks from riding (drawing by F. C. Yohn for *Collier's*, 1915).	106

INTRODUCTION

In her short story "The Artificial Nigger," Flannery O'Connor has an old man and his grandson encounter a rather interesting lawn ornament that neither of them has ever seen before or can begin to understand. As they stand mesmerized by the mysterious statue, the grandfather is compelled to offer some explanation and so he says to the child, "They ain't got enough real ones here. They got to have an artificial one."[1] The message that O'Connor wished to convey concerned the degree of ignorance that mid-twentieth century whites were prone to display when it came to the lives of African Americans, for the lawn statue holds absolutely no significance for the grandfather who nonetheless envisions himself a knowledgeable advisor.

Lawn jockeys have adorned the American landscape for over a century, particularly on the expansive plantation-style grounds of homes at various Southern locations. And yet the significance of those jockeys is not widely understood. For some observers, the statues may even seem ludicrous. Black men and boys in tapered uniforms, majestic in appearance as though about to embark on some magnificent task. Who would concoct such an image and then have it enshrined in the form of statues as if to celebrate some phenomenon that could never have occurred?

However, the fact of the matter is that the phenomenon did occur. From its earliest days to the present, American culture has partaken in the spectacle of various types of horseracing events. Indeed, in some circles the definition of a true gentleman included a knowledge of drinking, gambling, prizefighting, and horseracing. In those early days of the 1600s

Black lawn jockey (photograph by Monica Saunders).

and 1700s, the horse's actual owner was more likely than not to ride the animal in a given event. Virginians who migrated to settle into the Kentucky region placed high utilitarian value on their horses but were also fond of their participation in the racing competitions that grew to become the predominant sport of the times.

Williston Hough, in a 1905 *Outlook* magazine article, traced the origin of this sport from ancient times on into the Italian medieval era:

> The ancient Palii were more nearly like ordinary horse-races. Those run in honor of the Virgin Mary date from 1238, and were held at the Feast of the Assumption, on August 15. At first they were probably run outside the city walls, on some straight, broad country road. Later the race was through the streets of the city, from near one of the city gates to the Cathedral — a devious and dangerous course.[2]

Even in those early days, the races were public spectacles with a pageantry that was part and parcel of the social, and specifically the religious, festivities of the Italian localities. Such scenes were played out across the European continent, and as Hough, who witnessed one of those races in 1902, maintained, "The competitors have partisans and foes whose blood is hot with the loves and hates of centuries."³ Some of that fierceness between competitors had to do with how, over the centuries, the races evolved from being featured events in religious ceremonies to personal duels upon which huge sums of money were wagered.

By the second half of the seventeenth century in America, most of the larger towns in the East were building their own racing tracks. However, further west for almost another whole century, these competitions were held with horses barreling their way through the streets in the middle of town. In the early 1800s, formal racetracks were being built in and around the Louisville area, tracks such as the Hope Distillery Course, the Oakland Race Course, the Woodlawn Course, and the Beargrass Track, all having races that were conducted off and on for varied periods of time during the century as horseracing gained an even deeper foothold in the realm of sports and in the American psyche. Nevertheless, it was horseracing at Saratoga, New York, that had most captured the nation's attention. As one observer of the times put it, "It seems quite interesting as a great American sporting rendezvous, 'the greatest all round' resort of this sort we have yet evolved."⁴ Saratoga was flourishing in the mid-1800s while the Louisville racetracks were floundering in a fiscal depression reflective of what the city itself had been experiencing during the first few years of the 1870s.

That was when a young Louisvillian, M. Lewis Clark, took matters into his own hands and left for Europe, primarily to get ideas for the further development of racing in his own hometown. He left in 1872 and returned the next year after having visited with both the French and English Jockey Clubs. Clark was particularly impressed with the Epsom Derby, which had been held on the outskirts of London since 1780. The event had been founded by the 12th Earl of Derby, becoming so popular over the ensuing decades as to attract spectators numbering in the hundreds of thousands. In his account of that event for *Munsey's Magazine*, Hugh Logan declared that nothing on a par existed in America and the "owner of the winning horse carries with the blue ribbon a substantial stake ... and a reputation that will outlast that of kinds. The horse himself will be known by his progeny to the twentieth generation."⁵ It was that reputation that led Clark to try and reproduce a similar derby here on American soil.

Leasing land from his two uncles, John and Henry Churchill, Clark then gathered a small group of Louisville businessmen and incorporated the Louisville Jockey Club with the goal of developing a racetrack to both showcase the Kentucky breeding industry and attract the very best racehorses from around the country. The inaugural meeting at what was to become known as Churchill Downs was held on May 17, 1875, and a storied history was begun. As racing became more formalized, so did the delegation of related responsibilities. During slavery, blacks had usually been the ones who trained and cleaned up after their owners' horses. Now as racing was becoming more of an industry, the owners were enlisting diminutive African Americans to also do the riding. Needless to say, less weight on a horse's back meant faster times, and an especially strong and courageous jockey with a riding weight of 100 pounds might bring wealth and fame to a horse's owner, as opposed to a huge financial loss.

Not a few blacks in Africa had found themselves in a similar position just before being transplanted to these American shores. On the African continent, chiefs victorious in war often chose, from among their captors, those slaves most adept at handling horses. In his treatise *The Horse in West African History*, Robin Law informs that "the cutting and fetching of grass for horses, which was normally done by young boys, was regarded as an especially menial task, proverbially synonymous with the degradation and poverty of slavery."[6] Such was the state of affairs in America also, from the earliest days of slavery on into the twentieth century. The maintenance of horses had been considered a menial task that masters and then later, after slavery, horse owners in general did not feel they had to be bothered with in any direct sense. It was dirty work, but a job nonetheless that many blacks were already expert at as they transferred their knowledge from the African continent during the course of the Middle Passage.

As early as the late 1700s and early 1800s, some slaves were able to gain their freedom as a result of excellence in riding for their masters. Such was the case of "Monkey" Simon, only four feet six inches tall, but confident enough to issue a belligerent response to General Andrew Jackson who, at a race in 1806, warned the jockey, "Now, listen: none of your monkeyshines today. When my horse starts to pass you, don't you dare spit tobacco juice in his eyes—or in the eyes of my jockey. Understand?"[7] As the legend goes, Simon glared at the man who would eventually become president of the United States, spat to the side, and retorted, "General, I've rid ag'in many of yo' nags, but none ever got close enough to catch my spit."[8] There was nothing left for Jackson to argue since Simon was basically right and in those days when a race was close, it was not unusual for jockeys to whip at one another and use other such tactics that in more modern times would be considered a flagrant foul.

Simon could probably get away with more due to his small stature and enormous talent, and in addition he was a hunchback which perhaps

Black stable hands relaxing between working hours (*Outing*, 1902).

allowed him to take even more liberties with Jackson than what the ordinary black person would have taken with a white man, especially one of Jackson's stature. That jockey would go on to beat Jackson's horses on nine different occasions but would then die in relative obscurity, remembered for the most part only by some oldtimers in the Cumberland Valley of Tennessee. Writer Edward Hotaling observes:

> He died in the cholera epidemic that swept the middle basin of Tennessee in 1833.... In June of that year, the Tennessee newspaper noted that there had been sixty-two burials in a sixteen-day period. Simon's name was among those listed in the death toll for three days in Nashville. Interestingly, the list did not identify him as a slave, suggesting that, even if he had not been formally emancipated, he perhaps no longer lived as a slave—perhaps his technical status as a slave had become irrelevant, and he had simply become a town character, long since on his own.[9]

On June 19, 1833, the actual obituary printed in the *Knoxville Republican* was one that listed numerous victims of the epidemic, generally specifying the status of the blacks who were named, whether slave or free or free but employed in the service of a white individual. Simon's status was left vague in that obituary, indeed representing the anomaly that existed for some of the most successful black jockeys even while slavery was otherwise firmly entrenched in Southern society.

Six years after Simon's death, another slave would ride in what might be regarded as a preview for the race that would come to be known as the Kentucky Derby. That slave's name was Cato, and he would be riding a five-year-old Virginia-bred horse named Wagner. His stiffest opposition would come from a four-year-old steed named Grey Eagle who at the time was the pride of Kentucky and was to be ridden by Stephen Welch. There were originally 10 horses scheduled for this Louisville competition; however, six of the horses were dropped from the card, leaving only the two aforementioned entries and Hawk-Eye and Queen Mary, one of whom would remain in the competition for only one heat while the other would likewise pose very little threat.

Cato rode a strategically brilliant race, staying ahead of Grey Eagle for most of the race, only letting him gain ground toward the end. By the homestretch it was Wagner and Grey Eagle neck and neck pounding out the final 600 yards. Cato at this point forced Grey Eagle to the outside of the track, giving Wagner just the space he needed to bring home a victory in that first four-mile heat.

Shortly thereafter, the second four-mile heat began and again the race was a tight one between Wagner and Grey Eagle. Sensing exactly when his horse would need to get a second wind, Cato at first rode him hard, then let up on him some, and then pushed him hard once again until the two horses were neck and neck. And they ran like this all the way to the finish line with Wagner finally winning by a neck in a time of 7:44. It had been an historic race receiving national attention with Henry Clay and other prominent figures in attendance. As for Cato, he remains, in much the same manner as Simon, a human ambiguity without so much as even a last name for history to consider. Legend has it that upon winning that 1839 race he subsequently gained his freedom. But was it that particular race that won him his freedom, or the accumulation of oddities accruing to the very best of the antebellum Southern black jockeys? The very fact that they could voluntarily enter into contracts with white men, and then cross state lines to race those horses, rendered them a unique social status far beyond what the typical slave was allowed.

By 1875, there was even more prestige associated with being a jockey, but a prestige accorded to black jockeys within the context of a segregated world that still viewed blacks generally in the lowest terms. So when the first Kentucky Derby in history was run that year, it was not even regarded as extraordinary that of the 15 jockeys who rode in that event, 13 were African American. Such was the type of work that certain blacks did. No one in their wildest dreams could have imagined the incredible historical significance.

Introduction

Churchill Downs in 1903 (courtesy of the Keeneland Library).

It speaks volumes that the first jockey ever to win a Kentucky Derby was black, and yet he never rode in that event again. Down through the years, there would be 11 more African Americans to win the event, acquiring in the process varying degrees of fortune and fame. Some, such as "Babe" Hurd and Erskine Henderson, rode in the Derby and then faded into obscurity. Others, such as Isaac Murphy and Jimmy Winkfield, were able to develop such incredible careers that even the limitations of a racist society could not forever shroud the import of their greatness.

These jockeys, who began their careers doing all of the menial tasks associated with the upkeep of a rural horse farm, helped lay the foundation, and perhaps provided the most important element, for what was to become one of the most significant events in American sporting culture. Some, including Murphy and James "Soup" Perkins, paid a dear price, dying while they were still young men, having endured all the extreme dieting that their bodies could handle in their struggle to maintain a weight that would allow them to keep on riding.

The Kentucky Derby had not nearly the reputation then that it has today with its attendance mark of over 150,000 and millions more watching on television. In the early days, a crowd of 15,000 or 20,000 was considered a remarkable number. In those closing decades of the nineteenth century and on into the first few years of the twentieth century, spectators got to see a combination of the greatest jockeys and the very best horses in a race that has become the most heralded American horseracing event of the year.

CHAPTER I

OLIVER LEWIS
May 17, 1875

During the years 1915 and 1916, author Charles E. Van Loan published a series of short stories about a horse owner, Old Man Curry, and his jockey, Moseby Jones, who time and again raced that owner's mounts to victory. In one of those stories, "Leveling with Elisha," Van Loan presents the following conversation which entails Curry issuing instructions to Jones:

> "I want Elijah out there in front when you turn for home. With his early speed, he ought to be leading into the stretch. Elisha will come from behind ... and—you know the rest."
> Mose nodded soberly. "Sutny do, boss. But I neveh knowed 'at ol' 'Lisha—"
> "That'll do," said Old Man Curry sternly. "There's lots of things you don't know, Mose."
> "Yes, suh," said the little negro, subsiding. "Quite a many."[1]

That exchange is significant as it personifies not only what the nature of relations between blacks and whites were generally for much of this country's history, but it also more particularly characterizes what was the nature of relationships between racehorse owners and their jockeys during the latter part of the nineteenth century. It was typically the case in Van Loan's horseracing stories that Jones would be referred to as "little Mose," "my

Charles E. Van Loan's short story characters Moseby Jones and Old Man Curry plotting strategy (drawing by F. C. Yohn for *Collier's*, 1915).

little nigger," or "the bullet-headed little nigger," while Old Man Curry on the other hand was characterized as "the patriarch," wise beyond words in his dealings with people, especially on the horseracing circuit.

Just as Curry was so often given credit for the horseracing victories in Van Loan's stories, H. Price McGrath, the owner of the first Kentucky Derby winner, Aristides, is given primary credit for victory in that dramatic inaugural race. In actuality, it was a miscalculation on McGrath's part that led to Oliver Lewis becoming the first jockey to win in that event. Besides Aristides, McGrath had entered another horse in the race, a bay horse named Chesapeake who was physically a much more imposing animal than Aristides. In his autobiography, *Down the Stretch*, Matt J. Winn remembers, "Before the race started I had come to believe that Chesapeake was the greatest race horse in all the world.... He was a big fellow, he looked powerful."[2]

Indeed, McGrath had anticipated that if either of his horses could win, it would be Chesapeake. So he accordingly instructed Lewis to push Aristides hard at the beginning to in essence serve as a "rabbit" to wear down the rest of the field and pave the way for Chesapeake to surge forward at the end and claim victory. That strategy over the course of a one-and-a-half-mile race was designed to turn the likelihood of Chesapeake's victory into a virtual certainty.

Suffice it to say, Chesapeake's rider would also have had to have been a formidable athlete in order to make McGrath's strategy work. That other rider was another black jockey named William Henry. Yet history has recorded more about McGrath than it has about those two jockeys themselves who actually vied against one another for the Derby crown. Born in poverty in Kentucky, McGrath became a riverboat gambler on the Ohio and Mississippi Rivers before joining the 1849 Gold Rush to California and then venturing back to New York where he opened a gambling house. As George B. Leach reports in *The Kentucky Derby Diamond Jubilee*, it was at the point when he won $105,000 in a single night that he closed down his gambling house and returned to Kentucky, establishing the McGrathiana farm near Lexington where he settled into the occupation of breeding horses for what was essentially the rest of his life.[3]

McGrathiana was typical of the early great horse farms in Kentucky, an extension of the Southern plantation system. Historian Betty Borries further explains the dynamics of the system as it was responsible for the development of the core of America's early jockeys, including Oliver Lewis:

> It was common practice for a black mother to bring her child or children to her employer's home. In a truly agricultural society, such as the South formerly was, there were opportunities for play about the farms. As a child began to mature, a trainer might take notice of his agility.... The result would be a simple start in the role he would later assume as a jockey. True, they commenced usually by doing the tasks small boys could handle, progressing to exercise boy.... Most of our jockeys in the early years of thoroughbred racing were the products of rural life. Turfmen were constantly watching for promising boys.[4]

And indeed that is what the early jockeys were—boys. Playing and working around the stables from their earliest years, they were often exercising these powerful horses by the time they were 10 or 11 years old. They slept in the stables, took care of the horses, and consequently developed instincts about the animals in a manner that no other process could have accomplished so effectively. The work was dirty and in essence the same sort of work that slaves had done just a few years earlier. As far as those farms were concerned, not much had changed at all in spite of the Emancipation Proclamation. Theoretically, the slaves had been freed, but actual circumstances still resembled the antebellum period.

So, while McGrath and his horse Aristides became internationally famous, Oliver Lewis faded into relative obscurity. We know more about the heritage and lifetime of the horse than we do about the jockey who

McGrathiana, home of H. Price McGrath, who owned Aristides, winner of the first Kentucky Derby in 1875 (*Outing*, 1900).

rode him to victory. Barely over 15 hands tall, Aristides was "royally bred. He was by Leamington, the fine imported English stallion, out of Sarong, she in turn by Lexington. Leamington would also sire Pierre Lorillard's Iroquois, the first American winner of the Derby Stakes at Epsom, in 1881."[5] In fact, we can trace Aristides' ancestry back much further than Leamington. The Kentucky Derby's first winning horse's grandsire was Faugh-a-Ballagh; his great-grandsire was Sir Hercules. Unfortunately, no such line of ancestry exists for the jockey Lewis.

Little is known about most of the young men and boys who rode the horses in that first Derby. Conventional wisdom had long held that of the 15 riders, 14 of them were black. That is the assertion that Arthur Ashe made in his history of the African American black athlete entitled *A Hard Road to Glory*, as did Peter Chew who in his definitive study, *The Kentucky Derby: The First 100 Years*, declared that "Billy Lakeland on Ascension was the only white jockey in the Derby field."[6] However, the

Exercise boy, a job once held primarily by blacks (*Outing*, 1908).

author Edward Hotaling is of a different opinion, maintaining, "It is often reported that 14 of the 15 riders in the first Derby were African-Americans. Not true; at least two, Billy Lakeland and Cyrus Holloway, were white."[7] Chew and Ashe were writing in 1974 and 1988, respectively, whereas Hotaling drew his conclusion in 1996. One reason for the discrepancy can be attributed to the length of time which had passed since that first Derby. But at least equally as important as whether or not the number was 13 or 14 is that the number of blacks was not even deemed a significant feature of that first race whose very place in history had yet to be ascertained. Such is the nature of the difficulty involved in assessing the African American presence, especially in the earliest Derby races.

Most Kentucky Derby scholars give McGrath the primary credit for Aristides winning the 1875 Derby, as opposed to the jockey Oliver Lewis himself. In his 1903 analysis of horseracing, Charles Belmont Davis gave the following assessment of the situation as pertains to jockeys in general: "He is an insignificant ungrammatical-talking little tough ... a cringing servant to his employer and the club-house set. Brought up from his earliest youth in a stable, his whole life spent with stable hands and horses, generally without any education whatever, frequently broken in health."[8] Davis rendered that perspective in 1903, when blacks had all but faded from the thoroughbred racing scene. So, if his characterization pertains to jockeys at the turn of the twentieth century, it is logical to assume that Lewis' circumstances in 1875, in terms of what the possibilities were for receiving full recognition, were even more tenuous than they were for the jockeys to whom Davis would refer more than a quarter of a century later.

As we read accounts of how the first Kentucky Derby proceeded, there remains the question of who really most deserves credit for the victory. Quoting from the May 22, 1875, issue of *Spirit of the Times*, Leach gives us the following version:

> The horses got off at the first attempt, Chesapeake being one of the last to get away. Volcano made the running, closely attended by Verdigris, Aristides, and McCreery, the rest well together, a length or two behind. They ran thus through out the first half mile ... but the pace then began to tell on some of the rear division, and Enlister, Vagabond, and Chesapeake fell back. Aristides took second place as they ran along the backstretch, lapped Volcano as they reached the half-mile pole, the starting point ... and showed in front directly afterwards. The tremendous pace had already told a tale upon the field, which was now strung out a hundred yards behind. Chesapeake and Enlister being conspicuously in the rear. Aristides was steadily increasing his lead, Howard having taken a steadying pull on Volcano for a final effort.
> At the head of the stretch stood Mr. McGrath, who waved to Lewis, the rider of Aristides, to "go on," and he at once obeyed instructions by loosing his pull on his horse's bridle. Half way home, Volcano came with a determined rush, but Aristides stalled off the challenge in gallant style, and went over to score a winner of the first Kentucky by a length from Volcano.[9]

While McGrath had anticipated that his bigger and presumably stronger horse Chesapeake had the better chance of winning as between the two horses that he had entered, Oliver Lewis on Aristides set such a blistering pace as the "rabbit" that by the one-mile pole, only a few of the other horses had a chance of beating him, with Chesapeake having virtually no chance at all. McGrath's original plan had failed, and yet he still became the stuff of legend. The May 18, 1875, *Courier-Journal* reported, "Fortunately ... McGrath was near the head of the stretch, and taking in the position of affairs at a glance, waved his hand for Lewis to go on with the good little red horse and win if he could all alone."[10] The *Courier-Journal*, the *Spirit of the Times*, and other periodicals applauded McGrath for his good luck and his racing astuteness.

However, upon reading Lynn S. Renau's *Racing Around Kentucky*, another picture takes shape. That historian maintains that McGrath "always sounded patronizing in newspaper interviews as he referred to 'my darkies and my horses', which he openly admitted he ran into the ground."[11] According to Renau, the owner seems not to have had too much consideration for his black employees or for his horses, even while he loved the sport of horseracing. What McGrath loved most was the lifestyle that resulted from winning enough times to support his various and sundry activities at McGrathiana, many of them social.

Charles Davis pointed to the broad diversity of racehorse owners of that era, declaring, "Some of them have gone into the business just as they would open a livery stable; others because they love to own a good, honest horse; others because they have a great deal of money to spend, and they like to bask in the reflected glory of the success of the thoroughbreds running in their colors."[12] There existed then, as there does today, a certain type of pride in ownership and competing that has evolved into the extraordinary culture surrounding what has come to be regarded, in terms of the Derby itself, as the most exciting two minutes in all of sports. But as far as the credit for winning was concerned, Davis contended, "The credit really belongs to the horse and jockey and trainer."[13] And, one would assume, in precisely that order of importance.

Oliver Lewis (courtesy of the Keeneland Library).

Slaves were responsible for the daily maintenance of horses on the plantations of the American South. But the relationship between blacks and horses is one that extends, as mentioned in the introduction, much farther back in time. In *The Horse in West African History*, Robin Law cites 1675 B.C. as the date of the earliest presence of horses in Africa.[14] Slaves on that continent were charged with the responsibility of caring for the animals, particularly in the stables of African royalty. Moreover, during wartime, African warriors in certain regions were so dependent on horses that those animals could often mean the difference between victory and defeat. And during peacetime, horses where available were utilized for an extremely wide variety of purposes, from hauling to plowing, from sport to even food when the circumstances were dire enough to warrant it.

Considering that heritage, it is worthwhile to consider if Renau's assessment of the first Kentucky Derby victory is not the most accurate. She states, "Ansel probably put African American Oliver Lewis on Aristides for the first Derby with good reason. Lewis' expert riding saved the day for McGrath after Aristides' highly favored stablemate Chesapeake fizzled."[15] It is important here to reflect back to times of slavery when anything that a slave did was credited to that slave's master. For example, if a slave were to conceive a startling new invention, that invention would belong to the master. Eli Whitney gained fame for having invented the cotton gin, but there is serious question as to whether or not he was the one who did the inventing or whether by virtue of having been the owner of the person who did, the master thereby obtained credit. Such was the system in those days. By the time of the first Derby, only 12 years after slavery had legally ended, we are left with the question of just how much that system had changed.

McGrath is said to have shouted to Lewis, "Go on!" once that owner determined that William Henry riding Chesapeake had no chance of winning. Yet, Renau urges us to consider that it was Ansel who put Lewis on Aristides "with good reason." Who was Ansel? For a long time he was listed in racing records as "A. Anderson," not so much because "Anderson" was absolutely understood to have been his last name, but since "Ansel" was a Southern diminutive for "Anderson," publicists were simply doubling the name "Ansel" so as to provide this great trainer with some sort of last name. As it turns out, his last name was actually "Williamson." Born into slavery in Virginia in 1806, he was sold from one master to another, training horses until Kentucky breeder Robert A. Alexander bought and then finally freed him.

Williamson, however, continued working for Alexander until the latter's death in 1867, whereupon that trainer then went to work at McGrathiana, where he developed young boys into seasoned jockeys and produced great winning racehorses such as Tom Bowling and, of course, Aristides. McGrath, as Renau points out, "had none of Alexander's refinement or knowledge of pedigree but he had fortune enough to purchase Alexander's Thoroughbreds."[16] There at McGrathiana, it was Williamson who seems to have had the greatest amount of expertise when it came to racing horses, and he passed those skills on to certain young black jockeys, of which Oliver Lewis was one.

But even as he won that first Kentucky Derby, he was simultaneously involved in a struggle to raise himself and other black jockeys—and indeed blacks in general—from the depths of anonymity. Peter Chew describes "coal wagons packed tight with Negroes" who arrived on the grounds of the Louisville Jockey Club only to be crammed onto the inner field with virtually no chance of actually seeing the race. "Beneath the grandstand," continues Chew, "black women in bandannas and long-aproned skirts prepared corn bread, fried fish, fried chicken, and burgoo."[17]

Those black women were not included in the *Courier-Journal*'s depiction of the majestic throng of:

a thousand women ... exemplifying in her own enchanting face that
> —loveliness, ever in motion, which plays
> Like the light upon Autumn's soft, shady days,
> Now here and now there, giving warmth as it flies
> From the lips to the cheeks, from the cheeks to the eyes.

In the general effect of this grouping ... they blend into a general harmony.[18]

The "ladies" in the grandstand, dressed in their finest attire, combined to form a spectacle that has helped characterize the Derby from its inception up to the present day.

Comparable to that display was the attention accorded to the winning horse. In its next-day coverage of the Derby, the *Courier-Journal* had this to say about Aristides:

> Is there sense and sentiment in the magnificent animal? Else why his gleaming eye, and proudly arching neck, and plunging prance.... [H]is fame has been flashed across hundreds of wires before this, and has even traversed the thousand miles under ocean to be heralded to-day in every print read in the English language.[19]

Those accolades are appropriate, for it was the horse that did most of the work. But almost as important was the jockey who rode the horse to victory. It was Lewis who directed Aristides into the lead, Lewis who gauged the horse in what would be the fastest pace in one-and-a-half-mile racing history, Lewis who fended off the fierce challenges of Volcano and Verdigris. But Lewis' accomplishments were given short shrift in the wake of McGrath's command to "Go on!" And in the *Courier-Journal*, the trainer, by any name, was never even mentioned.

If Lewis had not won the Kentucky Derby he would have slid even further into the abyss of neglected history. The record keepers have sometimes seemed not even all that concerned to know which jockey rode which horse. Chew at one point in his book says that H. Chambers was riding on the runner-up, Volcano. At another point in the same text, that author claims it was a rider named Howard Williams. (Other sources confirm that Williams was the rider.) Similar errors have been made concerning who was the rider of the third-place finisher. If such was the fate of the riders of the first three horses to cross the finish line, than just how much can be certain about who rode which horse among the other 12 finishers?

Even Lewis' margin of victory is left somewhat to conjecture. Some sources say he won by a length. Others say two lengths. And what about after the Derby? What did he do then? Actually, Lewis was a much greater jockey than what the Derby victory alone might convey. It seems that he was something of a utility rider at the inaugural Louisville Jockey Club races which included the Derby; he won two other races that day. Churchill Downs reports that afterwards he worked for a bookmaker. For a while he was also a trainer in Lexington. But the details of his later life are sketchy as are the years leading up to his momentous Derby ride.

One month after he had won the 1875 Derby, Lewis almost won the Belmont Stakes at Jerome Park. Riding aboard Aristides, he was again set up as the rabbit but it was all he could do to hold the horse back from winning this race too. Even with the crowd shouting for him to let the horse go full speed, he continued to pull hard on the reins just as Price McGrath had instructed him. In assessing that race, Hotaling describes how "McGrath's Calvin, with Bobby Swim up, won as intended, the owner collecting thirty thousand dollars in bets. McGrath did prefer the more experienced Swim, so it was Bobby who rode Aristides to victory in the important Jerome and the Withers Stakes in New York."[20] Although Lewis had won the Kentucky Derby and come close to winning the Belmont Stakes—both of those races on Aristides—it seems that the typical plan for him was not to win but instead be part of a strategy whereupon others riding for the same stable would be set up to win, with Lewis assisting in their victories by pushing his own horse hard so early in the competition that any prospect of him winning was against the odds.

Perhaps the most profound reality is evidenced as Churchill Downs dignitary Matt Winn in 1944 declared, "I had seen every running since the first in 1875. Derby Day always had been the great festival day in Louisville; the one we all looked forward to as reunion time with old friends ... all of it climaxed by the race itself."[21] Winn had not missed a race in 69 years. It was his annual opportunity to renew old friendships and revel in the glories that combined to make the Derby one of the most spectacular events in sports history. Conversely, of Oliver Lewis it has been said that he was spotted at the Derby in 1907, 32 years after his own breathtaking ride. The report was made as though his appearance there was an extraordinary occurrence. But why should his presence at the track in 1907 have been regarded as such an unusual happening? Had he attended previous Derbies and just not been noticed? Or had he intentionally stayed away so long because of some discomfort that he had about the race, a discomfort that he had briefly set aside in 1907 to reflect on what he had accomplished just one generation earlier.

CHAPTER II

WILLIAM WALKER
May 22, 1877

Walker was born into slavery in 1860, on a farm in Woodford County, Kentucky. By the time he was 11 years old in 1871, he had already won his first official race, at Jerome Park in Westchester County, New York. At age 13, he was already a seasoned racing veteran, and two years later, in 1875, he was one of the entries in the first Kentucky Derby where he rode Bob Wooley to a respectable fourth-place finish out of the field of 15. It would be the first of four Kentucky Derby races that Walker would participate in over the course of a 21-year period.

In the 1876 Derby, Walker did not fare so well on the entry he was riding, a horse owned by Dan Swigert named Bombay. Robert Swim rode Vagrant to a two-length victory while Walker managed only an eighth-place finish. But Walker was nevertheless developing a reputation that would soon catapult him into the forefront of American jockeys. This was the same year that the United States Army dispatched troops to the Little Bighorn River to subdue the Sioux chief Sitting Bull, which in the short term resulted in defeat for the United States military but in the long run changed the landscape of the American West, eventually leading to the disappearance of Native Americans from the open plains.

The following year, several dozen blacks were banished from Henry County in Kentucky after the allegation that a black man had "slandered the virtue" of a white woman. Commenting on that and similar incidents

William Walker (courtesy of Churchill Downs, Inc./Kinetic Corp.).

in his book *Racial Violence in Kentucky, 1865-1940,* George C. Wright notes, "The greatest number of Afro-Americans were forced to leave communities all over the commonwealth not because they were warned out of town after lynchings nor because they were involved in political activities, but because whites were determined to eliminate them from the workplace."[1] Especially during times and in locations where jobs were scarce, many whites resented blacks who were given employment with developing companies, particularly in the developing coal mining industry, even though as Wright further explains, "Once hired in the coalfields, the blacks were assigned the worst, most dangerous jobs and received the lowest pay."[2]

In addition to resentment over blacks being able to get those mining jobs, there were whites in Kentucky, and indeed throughout the postbellum South, who resented black entrepreneurs who had been able to establish themselves in enterprises such as barbering, insurance, construction, and retail business. There was even some backlash against blacks who worked the land as sharecroppers and itinerant farmers, and of course the blacks who owned their own farms and were essentially self-sufficient. Yet in spite of all that, blacks maintained their position of dominance in terms of riding the best horses in what, over the course of time, would come to be regarded as the most important races.

By 1877, the Kentucky Derby was prominent enough to begin attracting dignitaries across a wide spectrum, from Kentucky Senator James Beck to Tennessee Secretary of State Charles Gibbs and the attorney general of Massachusetts, Joseph Ewalt. Also on hand was Dame Helena Modjeska, the famous Polish actress who was there in Louisville as the star of the American premiere of Henrik Ibsen's *A Doll's House.* Derby Day had acquired the status of Kentucky's pre-eminent holiday.

The pre-eminent American jockey was by now William Walker him-

II. William Walker

self. Says historian Betty Borries, "Until Isaac Murphy's rise to fame, he was the leading American rider. Having taught 'Ike' the rudiments of riding, he followed his career like a parent and was fond of relating all the elements of Murphy's prowess."[3] Interestingly enough, Walker's third Kentucky Derby in 1877 would be the first of eleven Kentucky Derbies for Murphy, the student who would win three of those races and place either second or third in another three Derbies, making him the most successful African American jockey to ever ride in the Derby. But in 1877, he was a 16-year-old boy going up against his teacher, Walker, who nevertheless was only one year older.

This would be a momentous race for another reason. Robert Swim, who had beaten Walker in the Kentucky Derby the year before, was aboard H. Price McGrath's horse Leonard. In fact, that entry of McGrath's was favored to win, and if that had occurred, it would have made Swim the winningest jockey in the Derby's thus far short 3-year history. Murphy, riding J. T. Williams' Vera Cruz, was also a heavy favorite. So, Walker certainly had his work cut out for him in a race that included Swim and Murphy in addition to eight other riders.

At the start of the race, the horses were bunched together, with the horse Leonard out in front by only a slight margin. Swim was pressing Leonard for every ounce of strength he could get while Walker held Baden-Baden steady in the fifth position. Having started poorly, Vera Cruz was now near the back. The *Courier-Journal* reported, "Vera Cruz had the worse of the start, and the simple fact of his being able to get fourth position when at the end of the half mile his backers thought him altogether out of the race, reflects credit upon the speed of the colt."[4] Vera Cruz was indeed a fast horse, but much of the credit for the fourth-place finish had to do with Murphy's skill at moving from near the rear of all the horses to almost near the front where he still had a chance of winning.

The real race would finally boil down to a battle between Leonard and Baden-Baden, the latter of which had been trained by the African American horseman Ed Brown. By the time the horses reached the backstretch, it was Leonard still out front with Baden-Baden in second place. At the three-quarter pole, Walker, according to the *Courier-Journal*, "gave Baden-Baden the word" and the horse responded, surging up alongside Leonard and passing him. Out of the final turn, Baden-Baden began plunging ahead for more ground, taking a commanding lead and winning by two lengths. In addition to the victory, the Louisville Jockey Club presented Walker with another award, that of being the "best behaved" jockey during the day's events.

Walker's reputation was soaring. Though he did not win the 1875

Edward Brown, trainer of 1877 Kentucky Derby winner Baden-Baden (courtesy of the Keeneland Library).

Derby, he was the leading rider at the Louisville Jockey Club track during the fall of that year. The following spring of 1876, he had been the leading rider once again, and yet again in the fall of that same year. By the time he finally won the Derby, he was already quite well known on the Louisville circuit. He tied with another jockey for leading rider in the spring of 1877, and would receive that honor twice more—at the spring meets of 1878 and 1881, the latter of which was another tie, but all in all, the number of times he was the leading jockey alone or tied for the award was phenomenal. Recognizing his greatness at the Jockey Club in particular, Churchill Downs, in 1996, searched and finally found Walker's unmarked grave in Louisville Cemetery and placed an overdue headstone there to commemorate his riding contributions.

It was on the Churchill Downs track that Walker participated in a race that at the time was deemed even more important than the Derby. Frank Harper's Ten Broeck was considered the best horse in the country at running particular types of races such as the match race, which pitted two horses against each other for distances ranging from one to four miles. While Kentuckians were proud of the famous Ten Broeck's reputation, Californians argued that Budd Doble's Mollie McCarthy was actually the greatest horse alive. As Matt Winn recalled, "Californians took exception and vowed that their Mollie McCarthy could run away any afternoon in the week from Ten Broeck and repeat it the next afternoon."[5] A match race was scheduled to take place on July 4, 1878, in which the two horses would race to see who could win the best two out of three four-mile heats. For the first two miles of the first heat, the horses were practically even and then, as Matt Winn tells it:

Mollie, seemingly fresh and strong, opened up a gap of nearly two lengths on the backstretch of the third mile, and Walker, deciding that this lead might be too risky, asked Ten Broeck to step it up. He tried with hand urging, but met no success. He gave him the whip—one slash, two, three slashes. But the gap remained....

Mollie McCarthy improved her lead to three lengths.... Was Ten Broeck through? Had he failed in this critical hour in his amazing career?[6]

As it turns out, Ten Broeck was not through. He overtook Mollie McCarthy in a "cyclonic charge" that gave him a 10-length lead as they finished the third mile. Ten Broeck continued increasing his lead until he had "distanced" Mollie, that is attained a lead so large that a second heat was deemed not even necessary to prove which was the better horse.

In addition to winning the Derby in 1877, Walker won the Dixie Handicap at Pimlico, Maryland, and during the course of Ten Broeck's amazing career it was usually Walker who did the riding. The jockey's career flourished on into the 1880s as he rode in races such as the St. Louis Derby and the Kenner Stakes at Saratoga, winning both of those races in 1882. And he remained one of the sport's leading riders throughout the 1880s and for much of the 1890s. A cruel irony is that less than three months before Walker—the teacher—saddled up to participate in the 22nd running of the Kentucky Derby, the student Isaac Murphy was dead from the rigors of racing though he was only 35 years old.

Riding in the 1896 Derby on William Wallace's The Winner, Walker at age 36 did not fare so well against the likes of Willie Simms, Thomas Britton, and "Monk" Overton. That year, Simms would win and though it would be the last Derby in which Walker would ride, he went on to have a successful career as an advisor for horse owners who found his expertise in bloodlines to be essential in the breeding of horses for the great turf races. John E. Madden, for example, employed Walker in that capacity and went on to breed five Kentucky Derby winners between the years 1914 and 1925. Having compiled that record, Madden became known as "the Wizard of the Turf," but the real wizard may indeed have been the 1877 winning Kentucky Derby jockey himself.

Walker saw 59 straight Derbies from the first one in 1875 to the one held in 1933, just months before his death on September 20, 1933. That was almost as many as the 70 that Louisville Jockey Club president Matt Winn had seen by the time he published his autobiographical *Down the Stretch* in 1945. It is unfortunate that Walker could not have been a member of that same club since he, throughout the decades, came to represent an important Derby tradition. In later years, he served as turf correspondent for various sporting publications, and he was able to die with the knowledge that, at least for a time, he was the best jockey riding on the thoroughbred racing circuit.

CHAPTER III

JAMES CARTER
May 21, 1878

Most sources maintain that 11 African American jockeys won a combined total of 15 Kentucky Derbies out of the first 28 that were ever run. During the years from 1875 to 1902, blacks won most of the Derbies and then black jockeys virtually disappeared from the racing scene. For three of those 11 jockeys there are no extant photographs or drawings to give us a sense of what they may have looked like. And then there is one jockey, beyond the aforementioned 11, who is even more of an enigma, mainly because he is hardly ever included as having won the Derby at all. His addition means that actually 16 of the first 28 Derbies were won by black Americans, and thus the collective contribution of those jockeys becomes even more profound.

The horse that was favored to win the 1878 Derby was a thoroughbred named Himyar, owned by Barak G. Thomas, Confederate Civil War veteran and sheriff of Fayette County. It was reported that:

> Himyar was a horse of great speed. W. O. Scully, whose White was third in the 1888 Derby, was taken to the track one morning before daybreak by Major Thomas who wanted him to see Himyar work. It was impossible to see the starting point of the workout. In order to time the horse, Thomas instructed a groom to strike the rail with a plank as the colt passed the starting point, saying that he would start his watch when he heard the sound. From out of the early morning fog raced a horse

past the finish wire. It was Himyar. [Then] from down the track came the sound of a plank hitting the rail.[1]

By that account, Himyar charging out of the fog actually beat the sound of the plank down the track. Such is the stuff of legend, but it is also a testament to the quality of horse that Carter would find himself up against.

As for his own mount in the 1878 Derby, Carter would be riding Day Star, who was bred by John M. Clay, the youngest son of Kentucky Senator Henry Clay. The elder Clay had been born in Virginia, but then moved to Lexington, Kentucky, where in addition to his political undertakings he acquired about 50 slaves, established Ashland Stud, and dabbled in the enterprise of breeding and racing horses. But it was the son who took the keener interest in horses at that plantation where "there was never a large number of mares and stallions ... but the quality of every animal was the best."[2] Indeed it was at Ashland that Henry Clay's grandson, Thomas Clay McDowell, bred Alan-a-Dale, who would go on to win the 1902 Kentucky Derby.

T. J. Nichols purchased Day Star from John Clay when the horse was still a yearling. Although he won no races as a two-year-old, he did win the Blue Ribbon Stakes at Lexington just a week before the Derby. The Derby itself would turn out to be a rather strange affair, all the more curious when Barak Thomas, suspecting that there might be foul play, took it upon himself to spend the night before the Derby sleeping in Himyar's stall, hoping that such a tactic would prevent any harm from coming to the horse.

It turns out that what the jockeys were capable of doing to each other and each other's horses during the race was just as critical as what someone might have done to Himyar the night before. Carter rode wisely just as the *Courier-Journal* reported. That newspaper proclaimed:

> Carter rode Day Star, and he jumped at his opportunity very cleverly.... Out of the dust ... just as the flag fell, could be seen a blue jacket streaking along the horizon. Day Star's colors were quickly recognized, while the dark solferino of Himyar's rider was seen pressing the squadron behind.... Carter saw his duty. It was to go with might and main, trusting simply to Providence.[3]

In the days leading up to the race, there was suspicion that some sort of impropriety might occur. Thomas had felt that there might be foul play in the stalls on the night before the race. In fact, something improper might have happened had he not been sleeping right beside his horse. But, as it turns out, the race itself was where questionable action took place,

III. James Carter

Ashland, the farm where John M. Clay bred 1878 Kentucky Derby winner Day Star (*Outing*, 1900).

something the jockeys must have anticipated because there were several false starts before the race was underway. When the dust finally settled from all that clamoring of hoofs just to get the race going, Carter could be observed pressing Day Star ahead while the blazing fast Himyar was only in fifth place.

Around the first turn, Carter was able to keep Day Star out front, but Himyar was struggling valiantly to catch up with the leader. Historian Jean Williams writes that Barak Thomas "had to stand by helplessly ... as Himyar was bumped by every horse in the race."[4] The crowd shouted out for Himyar, and almost as if in response to that cheer, he began passing one horse after another until only Day Star remained to be overtaken.

Down the homestretch Himyar was being whipped "cruelly" in an effort to gain the victory. Peter Chew asserts, "Jockey after jockey was heard to yell: 'Here he comes! Stop him.'"[5] Himyar was so "bumped and battered" that in spite of his extraordinary speed, he had been overextended physically in the process of extricating himself from the boxes that the other jockeys had set up for him. The fact that Carter was able to keep Day Star removed from that chaos for the duration of the race is the main reason that he ultimately won. Commenting on Day Star's courageous effort, George B. Leach declared, "His race in the Derby was described as the best race ever seen in America."[6] And Carter turned in a riding performance that contributed mightily to this phenomenal Derby upset.

CHAPTER IV

GEORGE GARRETT LEWIS
May 18, 1880

While some black jockeys achieved great fame during their lifetimes, such was not to be the case for George Lewis (Oliver Lewis' brother) who died while still a teenager, less than two months after his 1880 Derby victory. His July 10, 1880, obituary read:

> The colored jockey, Garrett Lewis, died at Hutchinson Station, Ky. on Monday, July 5th from internal injuries received in the mile heat race at St. Lewis [sic], Mo. June 8th, in which he rode the chestnut gelding Bravo who stumbled, fell and threw his jockey, Garrett Lewis who was stunned severely. Afterwards he recovered enough to ride a few races at Chicago, Ill. but had a relapse and died on his arrival home. He was a most excellent, obedient and good jockey and is a severe loss to the turf. He was in his eighteenth year.[1]

It is rather interesting how in that obituary, which first appeared in the *Thoroughbred Record*, there is no mention of Lewis' Kentucky Derby win which happened just a few weeks earlier. Perhaps it was because the Derby had not yet reached the stature whereby a victory there could be conceived as the single most important event in a jockey's professional life. And yet, in commenting on the make-up of the eight thousand people who came to see the Derby that year, the Louisville *Courier-Journal* announced that the crowd itself "has made Derby Day in America as famous in America as its English namesake is throughout the world."[2] The newspaper, in referring to the "English namesake" had reference of course to the Epsom Derby upon which the Kentucky Derby had been modeled. That latter event, by the early 1880s, had indeed become a relatively famous American race. However, the black jockeys who won those Derbies had yet to be accorded a comparable status in either racing circles or the overall society.

Significant also in that obituary is the characterization of Lewis as having been not only an excellent jockey but one who, in addition, was obedient. Lewis had been born during slavery and was another one of the many jockeys who got their start as a consequence of having grown up on a horse farm, labored in the stables, and subsequently acquired the necessary riding skills to compete in various races. As historian Lynn Renau states, "There was an understanding that being a jockey, for those who survived the experience, was a phase of a lifelong career with horses. When jockeys got too old or too big to ride they would join the ranks of trainers who developed horses for the boys that came after them. The system had worked that way for hundreds of years."[3] For all those years, it had been the plantation system in the South that had supported the horseracing phenomenon. During the time when Lewis rode, just a few years after slavery, that plantation system was virtually intact. Slavery had ended in a legal sense, but its vestiges still remained. Blacks had a well-defined place in the postbellum Southern culture. The positions they held were those based on a presumed inferiority that demanded not only deference, but indeed an absolute obedience. So it was only apropos for the times that in place of a listing of Lewis' next of kin, which would have been a quite difficult feat in itself, we have a commentary on what was in essence his role in an age-old social system.

The African American writer William Wells Brown understood the system well. Himself born on a plantation near Lexington, Kentucky, he escaped from slavery, and during the same year that Lewis won the Derby, published his collection of acerbic but wistful tales entitled *My Southern Home*. In that book, Brown tells the story of Joe Budge, who in his lifetime had 13 wives, 100 children, and at least 300 grandchildren. Budge, explaining his prodigious offspring, asserts, "You see, marser raised slaves fer de market, an' my stock ware called mightgood, kase I ware very strong, an' could do a heap of work."[4] When asked whether or not he could choose the women with whom he would have children, Budge explains further, "No, ser.... Marser allers get 'em, an' pick out strong, hearty young women.

Dat's de reason dat de planters wanted to get my children, Kase dey ware so helty."⁵

Those responses by Budge are Brown describing, in so many words, how some slave masters actually bred certain slaves with other slaves in an effort to build up a stock of the strongest slaves that could possibly be had. It was not so much unlike what the early Kentucky horse breeders were attempting to accomplish at their stud farms. In fact, Arthur Davis and Saunders Redding, in excerpting the above mentioned section of *My Southern Home* for their anthology *Cavalcade*, entitled the entry "Stud Negro" to reflect what they saw as the slave owner's general entrepreneurial intent.

Fonso, the 1880 Derby winner, was a product of the Woodburn Stud Farm, one of the most famous in all of Kentucky thoroughbred history. In 1876, King Alfonso was the primary stud at that farm, replacing the great racehorse Lexington, who had died the previous year. The next year, Fonso was born, a product of the mating between the mare Weatherwitch and King Alfonso himself. Then the following year Fonso was sold to J. S. Shawhan.

As a two-year-old, Fonso won three of the nine races in which he was entered. He placed second on two occasions and came in third in two other races. It was a good two-year-old outing by 1879 racing standards. The next year, Fonso began his three-year-old racing season by winning the Phoenix Stakes in Lexington. Other than the Kentucky Derby, he would race only once more in his career, during the fall season at the Viley Stakes in Lexington where he gained a second-place finish.

There were only five horses entered for the sixth running of the Kentucky Derby, but each one of them would, at some point in the race, challenge for the lead. At the outset, Lewis atop Fonso moved to the front, half a length ahead of Billy Lakeland on Kimball, the horse that had been favored to such an extent that the *Courier-Journal* reported, "So much had been said and written of Kimball ... that it was almost considered to be a foregone conclusion that he would win the race and win it in a canter."⁶ Lakeland had Kentucky Derby experience, having been one of the only two white riders in the inaugural race in 1875, aboard Ascension. Now he was holding firm in second place, just ahead of Isaac Murphy, who was riding Bancroft.

For Murphy, this was the third of what would eventually be 11 Kentucky Derby starts. In 1877, he had placed fourth on Vera Cruz out of a field of 11 horses. Two years later he came in second aboard Falsetto. Murphy must have figured that 1880 would finally be the year that he would win it all, finally finish first instead of just coming close to being the winner. Lewis was in front but he had the knowledge that right on his heels were Lakeland who was already something of a racing legend and Murphy who was well on his way toward legendary status too.

Boulevard was fourth and Quito last, that latter horse's jockey apparently playing a waiting game. This tactic of watching and waiting for other horses to burn themselves out was a rather normal strategy in earlier years, but now as racing distances had grown shorter, "they all ran at near-top speed from one end of the race to the other. But since a horse actually can spurt for only about three furlongs, the intelligence of the jockey became an important factor in knowing just how fast to run a horse, and still save a little extra energy for that battle down the homestretch. *He has a clock in his head* was a turf compliment."[7] Quito's jockey was trying his best to gauge how fast his horse could go this early in the race and still have a chance to win. The choice he made was to hold his horse back for a time even while Lewis, with Lakeland right behind him, was setting a rapid pace.

By the three quarters pole, Quito had moved into third place, ahead of Bancroft and Boulevard. Fonso still led and Kimball still held second. The waiting game strategy, though, was quickly becoming questionable due to the condition of the track. The *Courier-Journal* reported that "at the start the dust was flying so thick that the crowd did not fully realize the fact that they were off until almost the first quarter had been finished."[8] Jean Williams, in *Portraits in Roses*, maintains that "the sixth running of the Kentucky Derby was called the dust bowl.... The track was covered with dust ... making it nearly impossible for anyone to see the race—including the jockeys."[9] While the waiting game strategy might have been a good idea in other races, what was becoming more and more clear was that it was not going to be a good tactic this time. Lewis had wisely moved out front at the beginning and knowing how dry the track was, he was able to have Fonso kick dust into the eyes of his pursuers who at the first turn had much more to endure than just the dilemma of how to pace themselves. Fonso still led by a length over Kimball while Bancroft at this point had moved into the third position.

Up the backstretch, Quito charged past Bancroft to come within a head behind Kimball. Kimball meanwhile was fighting the dust (which by some accounts had risen to six inches high) and holding in second place behind Fonso, still the leader. Into the final turn, it was all Lewis could do to stay in front of Lakeland and then "into the finishing stretch, Kimball and Fonso were running neck and neck in the lead at a furious pace."[10] Kimball had been favored to win, but had he become far more exhausted than might otherwise have been the case had he not been right behind Fonso for so much of the race, in essence eating Fonso's dust?

Coming down the homestretch, it was anybody's race, and the jockeys knew it, for as the *Courier-Journal* reported, "Into the stretch all were whipping." Earlier while Kimball had been "catching the whip," Lewis was not whipping Fonso at all, which allowed the horse to keep on running easily even while the lead was being hotly contested. But by the final stretch, it was another matter as all the jockeys were pushing their horses to the utter limit. Murphy's Bancroft, who had been in third place early on, now fell all the way back into the last position and then ran fiercely to make it right back up into third place again. That was just how close the horses were as they approached the finish line.

Yet none of the other horses were able to overtake Fonso and Kimball. Lakeland whipped desperately. But Lewis, though in the midst of a maddening rush put on by the other horses, had not used his whip until the last one-eighth pole, when he gave Fonso a "touch of the whip" and didn't have to whip anymore as his horse surged forward to beat Kimball by a length. After the race, Lakeland rushed over to where the judges stood and he complained that Lewis had fouled him at the top of the homestretch, had bumped his horse and thrown him off balance so that he could not effectively challenge at that point. The judges, however, disallowed Lakeland's claim, and Lewis' victory stood.

It was a brilliant race that Lewis put on and he most assuredly would have had many more such victories had he not died at such a premature age. As remarkable as his Derby victory was, perhaps even more incredible was how he finished out his career even in the face of that impending death. Fatally injured in a race in St. Louis just a few weeks after the 1880 Derby, he continued to race for as long as he could until the only task that remained before him was to return to Kentucky to die at the place where he had been born.

CHAPTER V

"BABE" HURD
May 16, 1882

The early 1880s was an ominous time in America, particularly for the common laborer. In 1882 alone, 788,992 immigrants entered the United States.[1] The overwhelming majority of those immigrants had come here with the goal of some kind of employment, no matter how menial that work might be. The consequence of course was that many American citizens who were already here were having difficulty becoming gainfully employed. To help ease the crisis, Congress passed the Chinese Exclusion Act of 1882 to severely restrict Chinese immigration. But in spite of the Exclusion Act and other measures designed to limit Chinese participation in the American economy, Chinese immigration continued and employers continued to exploit the cheap labor pool.

Booker T. Washington saw the "writing on the wall" and in a speech that was actually a statement on behalf of blacks to all of America, he submitted that "in our humble way, we shall stand by you with a devotion that no foreigner can approach ... interlacing our industrial, commercial, civil, and religious life with yours in a way that shall make the interests of both races one."[2] Even as Washington spoke, he knew that it would be far into the future before the "civil" and "religious" affairs of blacks and whites would be substantially integrated. But he also understood what the effect of foreign labor would be on the employment prospects of blacks who had only recently been freed from slavery. It was a matter of one cheap labor pool in competition with another, and Washington was determined to do all he could to ensure that blacks, in their delicate economic position, would be somehow able to survive. Being fully appreciated was not at that point one of the leader's goals.

Relative to that history, Babe Hurd's position was somewhat unique. He had a job but it was within the postbellum plantation system where great appreciation was still not afforded black jockeys. Author Peter Chew has gone so far as to divide the Kentucky Derby into three distinct historical phases, asserting that "during the first period, purses were not high, but the race attracted crack horses ... who were to leave their stamp on the breed and succeeding Derby winners."[3] That first period to which Chew refers was from 1875 to 1898, a period of course in which black jockeys won most of the Derby races. The next period, from 1899 to 1914, is characterized by Chew as one of "mediocrity." As much as Chew may wish to make the distinction between periods based on a difference in types of horses, however, it was more than likely the case that the difference between earlier racing excellence and later mediocrity had to do with the difference in the skills of the jockeys who were virtually born into the sport and then allowed to disappear once riding horses became a more prominent and lucrative profession.

The irony indeed, as explained by one commentator, is that "increasing professionalism diminished black involvement."[4] Yet another observer assesses that "at first, racing people would push young black boys at an early age into the stables. They didn't realize they were doing the blacks a favor: they became the best riders and trainers."[5] Needless to say, the favor was largely unintentional. Hurd for a time was afforded a place in the plantation-type economic system and the author Betty Borries declares that he was a "well-known and successful jockey of the early 80's."[6] But so little else is known of his life, that one wonders just how successful his life really was beyond the Derby victory.

The 1882 event was Hurd's first and only Derby race. But the field was one of the larger, more competitive ones in Derby history. Erskine Henderson, a black jockey who would win the race a few years later in 1885, was now aboard Pat Malloy. William Lakeland, who had himself raced in two prior Kentucky Derbies, was now an owner whose entered horse was the highly regarded Babcock. And African American owner Milton Young had entered his horse Lost Cause in among the hopefuls.

Michael and Philip Dwyer, who had made a fortune in the meat packing business in New York City, owned Runnymede, who was favored to win this year. The president of the Louisville Jockey Club, M. Lewis

Clark, had been insistent on getting that particular horse in the race. As later Jockey Club President Matt Winn writes in *Down the Stretch*:

> Early in 1882, Clark asked Mike and Phil to run their 3 year old colt, Runnymede, in the Derby of that year. The Dwyers told him they would do so only if Clark would get some bookmakers into action on Derby Day. Clark said he couldn't provide any; that none was known to Kentucky. The Dwyers said they would bring their own.... Clark, wanting Runnymede, the star eastern 3 year old to run in the 1882 Derby, readily agreed to importation of bookmakers.[7]

Instead of the Derby, there were other more established races in which the Dwyers might have chosen to participate. Furthermore, another Dwyer horse, Hindoo, had won the Derby by a full four lengths the previous year and that earlier success gave the brothers additional leverage to dictate betting arrangements.

Though not favored to win the 1882 Derby, Hurd's mount did have a storied history. Apollo was a grandson of Lexington, famous in Kentucky racing circles for its phenomenal stud record—more than 600 colts and fillies including 260 race winners. In addition, Hurd's mount was a descendant of Diomed, the horse that won the very first Epsom Derby in England in 1780.

While Apollo did not race at all as a two-year-old, the following year as a three-year-old he would be the winner in three stakes races on three different tracks, all of those races occurring just prior to the Kentucky Derby itself. Those races were the Drummers Stakes in Little Rock, Arkansas; the Cottrell Stakes in New Orleans, Louisiana; and the Montgomery Stakes in Memphis, Tennessee. In spite of his phenomenal pre–Derby record though, Apollo was not expected to bring home the victory in Louisville.

There were quite a few excellent horses in this year's Derby field and the tension had mounted to such a level that two false starts occurred before the horses could get off fairly. Once they were off, it was the horse Harry Gilmore who "shot to the front as if propelled from a spring." Lakeland's Babcock was in second place and Pat Malloy, with Erskine Henderson riding, settled into third. By the first hundred yards, Runnymede was trapped in a pocket, and Hurd's horse Apollo was even further back near the rear.

Coming around the first turn, Babcock took the lead from Harry Gilmore, and Robert Bruce assumed third place, having gone ahead of Pat Malloy. Runnymede, at this point, broke out of the pocket where he had been boxed and now took over the fifth position. By the three-fourths-mile pole, Robert Bruce was advancing and moved out in front of Harry Gilmore by a head. Runnymede was in third, but still he was behind by a full six lengths. Babcock was fourth, Highflyer fifth, and Hurd on Apollo was in sixth position and completely out of contention, or so thought most of the spectators.

That crowd, however, would be in store for quite a surprise as:

> Hurd sat astride of Apollo cofident [sic] and waiting, saving his horse for the punishing finish. He was going carefully at sixth, and to the uniniti‑ated looked out of the race, but his rider's judgment was rare, and the fruition came in good time.[8]

The race became furious as Babcock, Harry Gilmore, and Robert Bruce contested for the lead. At the same time, Runnymede was boxed into yet "another dangerous pocket." Hurd, though seemingly out of the race as far as some were concerned, was not panicking but biding his time, watch‑ing the others jostling for position. Suddenly, Runnymede broke to the outside in an effort to catch the leaders, and by the one-mile pole, he had moved into third position behind Harry Gilmore and Babcock.

Further back, Hurd was beginning to make his move and "the white and purple of Apollo wove in and out between the orange, the blue, the red, the green, and the maroon of his struggling cotemporaries [sic], and flashed defiance in the faces of eleven of the choicest colts in all the land."[9] The race had been so chaotic early on that Hurd had had to wait patiently for the most opportune moment to make his move. With only a quarter of a mile left, Runnymede had taken the lead from Harry Gilmore, though only by a head. Still it seemed that, with such a short distance left, Run‑nymede was going to be the winner.

With just an eighth of a mile left in the race, Apollo, who had been weaving his way toward the front, now made a "cyclonic" charge until he and Runnymede were virtually even. The rider of Milton Young's horse, Lost Cause, had tried to follow Hurd as he wove in and out of horses to get up to the front. But Lost Cause's jockey could not keep up with Hurd's potentially deadly maneuver. The latter was riding in and out of the other horses so fast and suddenly that even efforts to box him in were unsuccessful. Continuing his charge, Hurd brought Apollo up alongside Runnymede just as they approached the finish line and won by half a length.

Before the race, analysts had concluded that Apollo could not win in a field of horses that was so highly touted. In fact, later that year, Apollo was again pitted against Runnymede, in the Clark Handicap in Louisville.

This time Runnymede won. But Hurd was not Apollo's rider, or else that race's outcome might have been the same as the Kentucky Derby result. After his thoroughbred racing career was over, Hurd did some steeplechase riding and then trained horses for Colonel W. V. Thraves at the Longridge Farm near Lexington. That farm was where the jockey died on December 7, 1928.

CHAPTER VI

ERSKINE "BABE" HENDERSON
May 14, 1885

The thoroughbred horse Joe Cotton would wind up being the third Kentucky Derby winner bred by A. J. Alexander of Woodford County, Kentucky. In all, between the years 1877 and 1901, Alexander was the breeder of five Derby winners, four of whom would be ridden by African American jockeys, including Erskine Henderson in 1885. Alexander, however, was not the original owner of the Woodburn Estate that produced such a large number of thoroughbred winners. During slavery that 4,200-acre farm had been owned by his brother, Robert Alexander, who was one of the richest men in the entire South before his untimely death in 1867, at 40 years of age.

That older brother was often referred to as "Lord Alexander" by his friends, a title given to him because of his extravagant lifestyle, which was comparable to that of a wealthy English gentleman. In his article on the development of the thoroughbred horse in Kentucky, Robert Woolley wrote of the older Alexander brother that "so lavish and imposing were some of his entertainments that the negroes for miles around thought he must be superhuman. They referred to him as 'Great Gawd Alexander.'"[1] His reputation for sponsoring grand events reminds one of H. Price McGrath, the first Kentucky Derby-winning horse owner. But with the advent of the Civil War, Robert Alexander was faced with the awesome challenge of holding on to his assets in the midst of marauding Union soldiers who were not averse to confiscating horses wherever they might find them. As E. Merton Coulter recapitulates in *The Civil War and Readjustment in Kentucky*:

> Fences were demolished, roads torn up, horses and other livestock taken.... As Kentucky was the happy hunting ground for those looking for horses, it became increasingly difficult for the owners to keep them.... By the end of 1864, Secretary Stanton ... ordered General Thomas "to seize and impress horses and every other species of property needed for the military services in your command."[2]

Robert Alexander had to sell, in addition to other horses, the legendary Lexington in order to keep them from being seized. He turned over another 34 horses to a friend, Harry Beland, who in turn sold some of them and entered others in races, eventually raising $300,000. And thus the farm was able to continue even as the war persisted. After the war, A. J. Alexander assumed ownership and that family enterprise returned to its pre–Civil War prominence.

It was on this farm that King Alfonso, the same horse that had sired 1880 Derby winner Fonso, also sired Joe Cotton. While still a yearling, Joe Cotton was then sold to J. T. Williams for $800, and though not particularly impressive as a two-year-old, he did go on to win his first four races as a three-year-old, including the 1885 Kentucky Derby. While not much is known about the life of Erskine Henderson, he continued to ride Joe Cotton after the Derby, winning the Coney Island Derby and Tennessee Derby the same year.

As had been the case with "Babe" Hurd, Henderson more than likely acquired "Babe" as a nickname due to the young age at which he began riding. In addition to his victory in the Kentucky Derby in 1885, he had ridden in that race two times before, aboard Pat Malloy in 1882, and Chatter in 1883. His first two Derby rides were while he was still a teenager, the first one when he was just 18 years old.

By 1885, he was a seasoned 21-year-old veteran, and he would need every bit of the expertise he had acquired over the years in order to pull out a win. It was anticipated that the Morris and Patton Stable would be entering as many as three or four horses, and that stable did actually have two entries, Berson and Favor, for whom was devised an elaborate plan not unlike what H. Price McGrath had intended in instructing Oliver Lewis on Aristides to act as the "rabbit" for the jockey William Henry on Chesapeake. In that latter case, we will recall that McGrath's plan fell through even though he still won the 1875 Derby largely due to Oliver Lewis' riding savvy. In the case of the Morris and Patton Stable in 1885, their plan would be thwarted by a jockey who was not one of their own, that jockey being Erskine Henderson.

The jockey riding Favor had been instructed to set a fast pace, and at the beginning of the race Favor was doing just that with Keokuk in second place and Irish Pat in third. Favor, however, was unable to keep the lead for long before Keokuk moved out in front of him. Meanwhile, Ed West aboard Berson had been instructed to hold his horse back and wait to see what Joe Cotton would do.

But something was going wrong with the Morris and Patton plan because Keokuk held on to the lead while Favor was falling further and further behind. Lord Coleridge moved into third place while Berson, who was supposed to be laying back, took over the second position. It was no longer West on Berson doing the waiting, but Henderson on Joe Cotton who was biding his time way back in seventh place.

Out of the first turn, as the horses reached the half-mile pole, Berson took over the lead and Favor was in second place but showing signs of exhaustion due to the all-out burst that he had undertaken at the beginning of the race. Meanwhile, Joe Cotton had moved up into third place. Henderson had had to be careful in advancing because some of the horses were being pocketed, but he was able to keep Joe Cotton out of danger while he and the other two leaders pocketed Thistle just as he had begun his charge toward the front.

While the first and second place jockeys were engaged in keeping Thistle from moving up, Henderson guided Joe Cotton into the lead. And so, coming out of the final turn and into the homestretch, it was Joe Cotton first and Berson second, with Favor holding on to third. Joe Cotton was holding the lead by only a neck. Interestingly enough, at this point, "some of the horses were catching the whip, but [Joe Cotton] was not, though Henderson was urging him with his knees."[3] The jockey had to be careful not to push Joe Cotton too hard and then have him fade before they reached the finish line. He held his narrow lead and anxiously monitored the situation.

Suddenly, Ten Booker made a whirlwind charge, passing Thistle and Favor and threatening to take the lead. But Ten Booker had been trapped at the back of the pack for so long that this last-ditch effort did not quite succeed. Henderson meanwhile was measuring just how much more he could draw from the exhausted Joe Cotton. And now he began to use whip and spur in the effort to hold off Berson. Two factors aided Henderson in his cause. One, West, on Berson, began his charge too late; and two, once West did begin his mad rush, Berson's own stablemate Favor was partially blocking the way. Still, even down to the last ten yards, the race was hotly contested between Joe Cotton and Berson until

> With both jockeys riding for all they knew how, Joe Cotton came first under the wire with Berson only a neck behind. Had Berson caught the whip at the eighth pole, and had he had a clear track, it seemed that he must have beaten Joe Cotton. Had the race been fifty yards longer Cotton would scarcely have held out. It was a close and exciting finish, in which every leap counted.[4]

Henderson had been measuring his horse for the entire race, staying within striking distance but holding back for just the right moment to mount his assault on the lead. And that had caused West to hold back too even though, in retrospect, his horse probably would have won the race had he spurred him on a bit earlier. On the other hand, Henderson's timing was perfect and his horse, though thoroughly exhausted, was able to hold off Berson and Ten Booker and win the race by a neck.

That same year that Henderson won the Derby, Kentucky was so embroiled in racial conflict that a special convention was held during which black leaders "denounced the discrimination the race encountered when appearing in court and the way the law consistently allowed white violence upon blacks to go unpunished."[5] Citing Louisville in particular, historian George Wright informs how blacks were systematically denied access to jury duty despite there being more than 28,000 blacks listed in the city directory, many of whom were prominent citizens, including quite a few businessmen, teachers, and other professionals. The white men who were responsible for jury selection had maintained that the "only reason why colored men were not placed on the list was because they were not acquainted with any who were qualified."[6] The excuse was an obvious lie designed to maintain white supremacy. But such tactics were typical of those times in which black inferiority was virtually taken for granted.

On the day before the 1885 Kentucky Derby, the atmosphere in Louisville was festive, as the following account depicts:

> Yesterday some twenty car-loads of brave steeds arrived at the Jockey Club grounds, and to-day others will come in. It is a noble assemblage, and a better lot of race horses was never gathered on a single course.... The horses were eagerly inspected, and mannerable questions were asked of everybody, from the President of the club down to the most ignorant stable boy.[7]

Just two decades after slavery, it is easy to comprehend how custom would grant greater status to the white president of the Louisville Jockey Club than to a black stable boy at the same location. The stable boys were deemed inferior because of their social status within the racing system, a status to which they were relegated due to the color of their skin.

Ironically, however, and contrary to most scientific opinions of the time, the stable boys and jockeys and trainers were far from ignorant. They may have been deprived of any formal education but, as Henderson's example shows, they were brilliant people and fascinatingly gifted horsemen. In fact Alex Perry, Joe Cotton's trainer, was black. Ten Booker, who nearly overcame Joe Cotton to win the Derby, was owned by Milton Young who, as mentioned earlier, bred and trained horses during an era in which the obstacles would have seemed insurmountable in terms of a black man accomplishing so much. Indeed if anyone should have been called "superhuman," it should not have been Robert Alexander, but instead individuals such as Milton Young and Erskine Henderson who actually developed and rode the steeds who were the staple of an illustrious Derby history.

In spite of his three Kentucky Derby appearances, little is known of Henderson's activities after he won in 1885, until 1913 when he was spotted once again at the Derby, this time as a trainer who as historian Lynn Renau avers was "still small enough to gallop his own horses."[8] What happened to Henderson in the intervening years? In his novel *God Sends Sunday*, Arna Bontemps tells the story of a black boy named Little Augie who was passing his time on a Southern plantation in the late 1800s when

> One spring ... the fancy Woodbine stable was hard pressed for jockeys, and Augie was put into the saddle to fill the need. Augie had looked forward to just such a day since the afternoon, then years past, when he had first wandered across the city to the Fair Grounds. He had come a long way to those dim sheds, and it had taken many years to achieve his dream after arriving.... [H]e realized ... that there was a grimmer angle to the business, an angle that he had failed to consider. He put the whip on Jennie Rose.... [O]ne by one, she broke the hearts of her rivals, running past them with a burst of speed that thrilled Little Augie like a vision of heaven.[9]

Little Augie won that race, but he was absolutely right in his observation that there was a "grimmer angle to the business." And "all of a sudden bad days came upon [him].... In the races his horses stumbled, wrenched their legs, or otherwise failed. Mr. Woody turned spiteful and assigned him to all the impossible mounts."[10] While that need not necessarily have been Henderson's history once his Kentucky Derby-riding days were over, it is worthwhile to consider the extent to which luck played a part in the lives of black jockeys who frequently were viewed as expendable. Just one defeat could be disastrous in terms of finance and opportunity. Henderson himself faded from the racing scene for an extended length of time, and one wonders what precisely were the limitations in his life at so early an age that caused him not to race in the Derby again after 1885. Whatever they were, he was just as Bontemps had declared of Little Augie, "no simpering pie-backed nigger.... He was a race-horse man."[11]

CHAPTER VII

ISAAC LEWIS
May 11, 1887

Like many black jockeys before him, Isaac Lewis was raised on a farm in rural Kentucky. Born in Bourbon County in 1870, it would not be long before he was riding horses, and by the time he was 11 years old he had won his first race. The horse that he rode in that race was a three-year-old black colt named Eniskillen, owned by H. Price McGrath. At the McGrathiana estate, African American trainer Byron McClelland had observed Lewis' affinity for horses and developed him while he was yet a boy. As a result of that mentoring, Lewis became an accomplished jockey before he was even a teenager. Upon the death of McGrath, the team of McClelland and Lewis worked for several other enterprises including the Calazzi Stables. The jockey was highly regarded for his ability to get his mounts off quickly, and he was also credited for his astounding fearlessness, driving those horses hard on the turns as if oblivious to any danger.

After the death of Price McGrath, Milton Young purchased the McGrathiana Stud Farm and continued in earnest the enterprise of breeding that the original owner had begun. Robert Woolley, writing in 1900, offered the following general history of the breeding of Kentucky thoroughbreds:

Breeding the thoroughbred was for years a luxury in the Blue Grass region, then it became a business, and now it is the most important industry there. The Kentucky gentleman was rich and he raced for the glory of winning; the civil war first caused him to breed and race more for money; recent reverses of various kinds have further hampered him financially, and now he is being supplanted as a breeder by the New York millionaire.[1]

Michael and Philip Dwyer were two examples of New Yorkers, to which Woolley refers, who supplanted some of the highly reputed Kentucky horse owners. But to fully comprehend the significance of Milton Young's involvement in the racing arena, it is useful to consider a poem entitled "This Is Not a Poem," written by contemporary scholar and Louisville native Houston A. Baker, Jr. In that poem, Baker conveys that a white person chastised his grandmother when her daughter (Baker's mother) referred to a black man as "gentleman."[2] Baker's poem is the recapitulation of a Depression-era situation in Louisville, so one can imagine what a feat it was for Young, in the 1880s, to enter into the realm of Kentucky gentlemen all the way up to the point of assuming the traditional Kentucky title of "Colonel."

There at McGrathiana, Young bred Montrose from the Duke of Montrose and Patti, "sire and dam," as the *Courier-Journal* put it, "being both fast and game." And one of Montrose's great-grandsires was Pat Malloy, which Erskine Henderson had ridden so ably in the 1882 Kentucky Derby. It is a well established fact that most of the Kentucky Derby-winning horses have evolved from very distinct and elite bloodlines. Young understood the nature of this thoroughbred development, bred his horses accordingly, and then sold them at a substantial profit. He sold Montrose to W. S. Barnes, who then resold him to the Labold Brothers Stable, who then engaged Isaac Lewis to ride him in the Derby.

Though he had not been favored to win the 1887 Kentucky Derby, Lewis was actually at something of an advantage, having a horse that was the result of such careful breeding by Young. As a two-year-old, Montrose won the Free Handicap and Cotton Exchange Stakes. He would later go on to win a whole host of other races including the St. Leger Stakes, the Blue Ribbon Stakes, the Morrissey Stakes, the Distillers and Brewers' Stakes, the Great Western Handicap, the Cincinnati Hotel Handicap, and the Kearney Stakes twice.

Yet it was another horse who was favored to win the Derby in 1887. The *Courier-Journal* declared that "Banburg, as the favorite, was most anxiously looked for, and as Blaylock rode the racy-looking gelding past the stand the crowd tendered him an ovation.... [I]n his preliminary

Isaac Lewis (courtesy of Churchill Downs, Inc./Kinetic Corp.).

gallop [he] gave evidence of that enormous stride which the knowing ones had said would bear him to certain victory."[3] The newspaper further reported that "[t]he Banburg tip was so strong and persistent that it seemed to take possession of the crowd and inoculate the book-makers."[4] This horse was such an overwhelming odds-on favorite to win that the crowd cheered wildly as he was paraded in front of the stands before the race had even begun.

Lewis faced further stiff competition from Isaac Murphy for whom this would be his seventh Kentucky Derby appearance. Riding Pendennis for the Santa Anita Stable, Murphy was also cheered as he passed the grandstand during pre-race introductions. Though Pendennis was a virtual unknown, he still was favored to come in third, based largely on the stellar reputation of Murphy. Lewis, whose horse was projected to finish sixth from among the seven that were entered, had raced against Murphy before, just one year earlier in the 1886 Derby. Neither of those jockeys won, however, with Murphy coming in fourth and Lewis sixth out of a ten-horse field.

VII. Isaac Lewis

Milton Young, breeder of 1887 Kentucky Derby winner Montrose (*Outing*, 1900).

While Lewis had honed his skills under the watchful eye of Byron McClelland, there was yet another distinguished black jockey in the 1887 race, one who ironically had developed under the tutelage of the same Milton Young who had bred the horse that Lewis would ride. John Stoval was born near Louisville in 1862, began riding at age 13, and then spent two years exercising horses at Midway, Kentucky, just outside of Lexington. When he was 15 years old he had started racing at major events, winning the Alexander Stakes on General Abe Buford's Goodnight in 1878, and riding that same owner's General Pike in the 1879 Kentucky Derby. Between 1879 and 1885, Stoval would ride in four Kentucky Derbies, placing third on Milton Young's Ten Booker in 1885, almost beating Erskine Henderson.

Stoval had begun riding for Young in 1880. He also rode for Edward Corrigan and Leonard Jerome, and then returned to ride for Young as well as other owners, winning 41 out of 119 races one year and 47 out of 215 races in another racing campaign. His most phenomenal day was on October 1, 1881, when he rode four winners in a single meet. After that feat the victories continued, including: the Alabama Stakes, Spinaway Stakes, and Kentucky Oaks in 1882; the Kentucky Oaks, Clipsetta Stakes, Clark Handicap, and St. Louis Derby in 1883; the Dixie Handicap in 1884; and the Kenner Stakes and Tennessee Oaks in 1885. In 1886, he raced aboard Lafitte in the Kentucky Derby, but failed to finish ahead of either Murphy or Lewis.

Now the stage was set for a rematch. Banburg was the favorite, but three wily veterans who had battled each other just one year earlier in this very same race were setting their sights on pulling off an upset. Stoval's strategy was simple. Go to the front and hold on to the lead. But all of the horses had gotten off to a good start, and Ban Yan and Montrose were especially quick in pursuit of Stoval's Jacobin.

Before the horses had even reached the first turn, Lewis aboard Montrose had assumed the lead. Ban Yan was in second. Murphy on Pendennis had pulled into third. Into the first turn, Lewis held a two-length lead and would hold the lead for the rest of the race. It seemed for a moment as though Lewis might pull away from the pack even further, making the race a rout, but then the other jockeys began closing in, pushing their horses, and "the racing had begun."

In the backstretch, Banburg moved up to challenge the leader. Jim Gore and Jacobin were also in hot pursuit. Still, Montrose held on in what had become a four-horse race. As they came out of the turn and into the final stretch, it was Montrose, Jim Gore, and Jacobin out in front. Lewis' horse had been picked to finish next to last, but now he was fighting gamely, holding on to the lead. Stoval tried to push Jacobin for more, but the horse had essentially spent all of his energy. The jockey on Jim Gore also tried to muster a last-ditch charge, but Lewis had Montrose in such a powerful, easy stride that all the challenges were to no avail.

Isaac Murphy had won the Derby in 1884. He participated again in 1885 and 1886, but was unsuccessful in those two bids. Now, in 1887, he was denied once more. It would take three more years for him to get a second Derby victory.

The year 1887 is also significant because it would be Stoval's final of six Kentucky Derby efforts. When he charged after Lewis on Montrose in the backstretch, he was chasing that horse and jockey, but he was also inadvertently chasing history. By falling short this final time and only placing third, he would join the ranks of some of the other black jockeys—Monk Overton, Jimmy Lee, Jess Conley, and Dale Austin—who raced multiple times in the Derby, but always without the victory. Stoval would go on to win the Latonia Cup in 1887, the Latonia Oaks in 1888, and the Kentucky Oaks and the United States Hotel Stakes in 1889. And then he met with a tragic death in 1900, when his horse fell down and crushed him in the middle of a race.

Lewis wound up winning the 1887 Derby by two lengths. That same day, he rode Brookful to victory in two separate heats of the Frank Fehr City Brewery Purse. He continued his riding career well into the 1890s, winning, in addition to other races, the Great Western Handicap in 1888, again aboard Montrose. In 1891, he won the Hyde Park Stakes and the Saratoga Cup. He would also ride in two more Kentucky Derbies, in 1888 and 1889, but placed only fifth and sixth, respectively.

CHAPTER VIII

ISAAC MURPHY

May 16, 1884; May 14, 1890; May 13, 1891

In his 1968 study on horseracing entitled *The Racing Game*, historian Marvin Scott assessed what he perceived as the unique presence of blacks in this particular sport. Scott asserted:

> When a Negro exercise boy is given opportunities to "don the silks" in the afternoon, he tries so hard to make a good showing that as a result he shows a lack of coolness. Interestingly, in the nineteenth century most jockeys were Negroes, and one of the reputed all-time greats was Isaac Murphy, a Negro. Horsemen acknowledge this, but contend that the style of racing has changed in such a way that qualities are called for today that were less important in an earlier day, qualities that are captured by the term "coolness."[1]

If there was ever an inappropriate statement about African American jockeys, Scott's evaluation is one such example because Murphy's style of riding was, if nothing else, the quintessential example of coolness. Famous for what some newsmen of the time referred to as his "Murfinishes," the jockey's primary technique was to hold his horse back and let other jockeys move out into the lead and set a pace as rapid as they wished. Eventually those leaders would tire and then Murphy would make his move, driving his horse to victory after having held enough in reserve to mount an effective surge near the end of the race.

So stoic and in control was Murphy, as he employed this strategy over and over again, that he garnered a reputation as a "wizard in the saddle," "the Sphinx," and an "excellent judge of pace" during what were his peak years in the late 1880s and early 1890s. Just for the two-year period of 1888 and 1889, he won 97 of the 254 races in which he competed. And over the course of his entire career, he amassed 628 victories out of the 1,412 races in which he rode. His winning percentage was .445, a record that will probably never be beaten. Eddie Arcaro, who would eventually win five Kentucky Derbies, only had a winning percentage of .22. Willie Shoemaker, who won the Derby four times, had a lifetime winning percentage of .24.

The careers of Arcaro and Shoemaker can be used as an earmark for the modern era of Kentucky Derby racing, covering the broad span of decades from the 1930s to the 1980s, aboard such mounts as Whirlaway and Citation in the case of Arcaro, and Lucky Debonair and Ferdinand in the instance of Shoemaker. In fact, by winning the Derby so many times, those two men have become racing legends of a sort that was not available for Murphy during the time in which he rode. Of course, the Derby was not as significant a race as it is now. During the years from 1884 to 1888, Murphy won Chicago's American Derby four out of five times, and that was a more significant accomplishment than his Kentucky Derby victories. He won racing events all over the country, from Saratoga to California and throughout the South, rising to the level of being the pre-eminent jockey of his era. Still, something important was missing. He could be a great jockey, perhaps the best who ever lived, but he could never be a national hero, even though horseracing was the dominant sporting event in America during his lifetime.

Murphy was born on January 1, 1861. Slavery still existed but Murphy's father, James Burns, was a freeman and bricklayer on David Tanner's Pleasant Green Hill Farm in Fayette County, Kentucky. Murphy's mother was a laundress for several families in the area. Young Murphy would never really get to know his father because once the Civil War broke out, Burns enlisted in the Union army and was later captured and taken to Camp Nelson, 21 miles south of Lexington. He died there, leaving his widow with two children—Isaac and a sister who herself would die while still in her early childhood.

After her husband's death, Murphy's mother continued working as a laundress for various families including the family of Richard Owings,

Isaac Murphy (courtesy of the Keeneland Library).

a partner with the Owings and Williams racing stable. As young Murphy (who at the time was still going by the name "Burns") grew up in the presence of the Owings household, it was becoming more and more obvious that he was in possession of the very attributes that made for excellent jockeyship—a short build with strong legs, long sinewy arms, and an affinity for horses. Owings brought the boy to his partner's attention and soon thereafter the child began his jockey apprenticeship.

Isaac Burns was only 12 years old when he was hoisted up on a yearling colt and instructed to begin breaking the horse in. Young Isaac did not last up on that horse very long before he was thrown off. That was his first riding experience and he quite understandably was reluctant to ride again. Nevertheless, he was persuaded to remount, and thus his education in horsemanship proceeded with great diligence until two years later, in May 1875, he won his first race aboard Lady Greenfield, in Louisville. While at the Owings and Williams Stable, Isaac came under the tutelage of African American trainer Eli Jordan who, in evaluating his student, maintained:

> Ike was always in his place and I could put my hand on him any time, day or night. He was always one of the first up in the morning, ready to do anything he was told to do or to help others. He was ever in good humor and liked to play; but he never neglected his work, but worked hard summer and winter. He never got the big head.[2]

The lessons from those early years would last the promising young jockey an entire lifetime, for beyond acquiring excellent skills in the saddle, he gained a reputation for having an incorruptible character. A handshake from Ike was as good as a written contract. If he promised an owner that he would ride a particular horse, then he kept that promise even if other owners later offered him more money to ride for them in that same race.

As his reputation for good riding and honesty became more widely known, the opportunities to cheat in some way or another became more pervasive. Many times, he was offered more money to throw a race than what he could have gotten from a victory. Yet he remained true to his conviction that such dealings would be a mistake, and he likewise advised other upcoming jockeys, telling one of them, "You just ride to win. They get you to pull a horse in a selling race, and when it comes to a stake race, they get Isaac to ride. A jockey that'll sell out to one man will sell out to another. Just be honest."[3] Ike understood well what the temptations were at all the racing levels, and early on he concluded that a jockey without integrity faced an uncertain future in the business even if he was a talented horseman. He did not gamble and until his later years he did not indulge in alcohol. He was the consummate athlete who, with his effervescent personality and drive to win, might in a later era have been an icon along the lines of what Muhammad Ali and Michael Jordan accomplished in their respective athletic fields.

That manner of conducting oneself with the utmost integrity made even more sense for a black jockey because

> Honesty and integrity would turn out to be their most important weapons for survival. If the black jockeys had a better reputation for integrity ... the explanations were several, but fairly simple. More of them had come up the hard way, which built character. Fewer had been exposed to the temptations of easy money, which weakened character. They had a lot more to lose. For them, any trouble was big trouble. If they were caught in a scam, they had reason to fear worse punishment than whites and would also find it harder than whites to get another job.[4]

With the sport gaining more and more prominence with larger and larger sums of money at stake and in an atmosphere where many jockeys were reverting to underhanded methods in order to win races at any cost, black jockeys understood that they were not afforded the same privilege. The stigma attached to blacks in general was that they were of an immoral nature. Many black jockeys sought to dispel stereotypes such as these— and the presumptions associated with them—in order to compete.

When her husband died, Ike's mother returned to her father's home in Lexington and so the grandchild, while in his formative years, had the benefit of his grandfather Green Murphy's wisdom and insight. In large amount due to that profound influence, Ike changed his last name to "Murphy" shortly after he began winning and kept the new name throughout his career. He must have had some sense of what the magnitude of his accomplishments would be and was thus dedicating his career to that grandfather who took his daughter back in with her two young children in their critical hour of need.

The 1877 season would be Murphy's first full season of riding and he all but took the racing world by storm, ultimately winning 19 of the 45 races in which he was entered. It was a remarkable start due largely to Vera Cruz, a bay gelding owned by Williams at the stable where Murphy had first learned to ride and where he would remain for a substantial period. On Vera Cruz he would win the Cumberland Stakes in Nashville and the St. Leger Stakes in Louisville. But the jockey was not meant to win the Kentucky Derby that year and could only bring Vera Cruz in with a fourth-place finish behind Billy Walker on the winner Baden-Baden and Bobby Swim on Leonard, the second-place finisher.

Murphy spent most of the following year riding for Williams until while racing at Chester Park in Cincinnati, he experienced a setback. Riding Classmate in that race, another jockey suddenly cut across him, almost causing serious injury to several other horses and their jockeys. One of those other jockeys subsequently struck the offending jockey across his face, causing blood to spatter everywhere, including on Murphy's shirt. After the race, the jockey who had cut across the other horses went to the judges and filed a charge against Murphy, claiming that he had struck him, and since Murphy was covered in blood, it looked like he had indeed been the perpetrator of a foul. Classmate was disqualified and Murphy himself was fined $25 and given a one-year suspension. The suspension, however, was lifted after a few months once it came to the attention of one of the judges that Murphy had been wrongly accused. Ike was back in the saddle before the year was out, winning more races for the growing number of owners who were vying for his services.

Horses bred in Kentucky had won the first four Kentucky Derbies. Now, the fifth Derby was being hailed as a contest between the states of Kentucky and Tennessee. A Tennessee thoroughbred, Lord Murphy, was favored to win, but the Kentucky-bred Falsetto was thought to be the horse, from among eight other entrees, that could give Lord Murphy the greatest challenge. Ike rode with great confidence and almost won, but surprisingly Lord Murphy was able to overcome being bumped almost to his knees early on and he came from behind to beat Falsetto by a length. Charles Shauer was the winning jockey that time, but in claiming second place, Murphy laid significant groundwork for future runs in this Louisville event.

The "dust bowl" Kentucky Derby of 1880 gave Murphy yet another opportunity. In that race, he rode Milton Young's Bancroft but was never able to advance beyond the third position. The black jockey George Lewis, riding Fonso, was able to hold off Billy Lakeland on Kimball, the horse that had been favored to win. Murphy, on the other hand, had to wait another four years for his first Kentucky Derby victory.

But he was winning virtually everywhere else. In 1881, he won 22 of the 49 races in which he was entered. The following year, he won 33 out of 88, finishing second 20 times and third another 10 times. It was coming to be understood that just having Ike aboard a given horse increased the odds of winning if the horse was any good at all. And usually his mounts were very good since his own reputation had grown to the point where he was offered only the best horses to ride.

By now, Murphy was quite well off financially and thus felt comfortable enough to propose to a young acquaintance of his, Lucy Osborn. They were married in 1882, and acquired various properties, particularly in the Lexington area. Though they never had children, they had many friends among whom was Anthony Hamilton, a black jockey from South Carolina whose wedding reception would be a gala event at the Murphys' Lexington home. Lynn Renau describes:

> The festivities began at noon and ended at midnight. Except for a smattering of doctors and a professor, the notables were all Derby-calibre riders—Isaac Lewis, Thomas Britton, William Walker (Murphy's life-long friend), Ed Brown, Raleigh Colston, George Smith and Hamilton, a South Carolina native who had trained under English jockey-turned-trainer William Lakeland. Hamilton later rode in Europe and died of consumption aboard his private railroad car in Germany, swathed in sable with rings glittering on every finger.[5]

Hamilton never won the Kentucky Derby but he was a much-feared rider during his 12-year career. His nickname, "the black demon," had its derogatory overtones and yet it captured the essence of what it was like to have to race against him on the track. Moreover, he and some of the other distinguished black jockeys joined with Murphy in something of an informal professional brotherhood.

Murphy's own career continued to develop and though he did not have a mount for the 1882 Kentucky Derby, he did get the chance to ride Apollo, that year's Derby winner, in other events including the United States Hotel Stakes and the Kenner Stakes, placing second both times in those races at Saratoga. Again in 1883, he missed the Derby but rode the Derby winner in eight other major stakes races, winning every time. It was not long before he became known in racing circles as the "colored Archer," in reference to England's Fred Archer, five-time winner of the Epsom Derby and regarded by most as the greatest rider in that country's entire racing history. Before his career was done, Archer would win a total of 2,748 races, more even than the African American James Winkfield, whose racing career spanned a period of time twice as long as that of the heralded Englishman.

As good as Archer was, some American turf reporters felt that it would have been an honor for Archer to have been called the "white Murphy." Archer had begun his career earlier than Murphy and accumulated many more victories, but in actuality he was not on a par with Murphy in terms of the integrity that was consistently displayed by the latter jockey in his interaction with the various horse owners and indeed the horses themselves. Peter Chew explains, "Archer was known as a 'tin-scraper,' meaning that money was an obsession with him, and when he rode, he punished his mounts severely with spur and whip. In this sense, he was quite unlike Murphy, who was as willing to ride for a poor owner as a rich one, and who was celebrated for sparing his horses, rarely using the whip."[6]

As has already been noted, Murphy valued honesty over money, and his ability to look out for his horse's well-being, while at the same time figuring out a way to win, was just one more aspect of his style that made him extraordinary. His manner of pacing a horse, so that the animal had enough energy near the end of the race to overtake the leader, was a skill that he came as close to perfecting as anyone else in the racing business. That he won practically half of all his races, using that style, is a testament to just how talented a jockey he was.

Murphy would face a stern test, though, with Buchanan in the 1884 Kentucky Derby. He was well aware of that horse's factious nature because he had ridden him several times during the previous year in races for two-year-olds. Buchanan had thrown the jockey before, and now at the Derby seemed absolutely uncontrollable. He threw Murphy off before the race had even begun, prompting Murphy, who knew all too well the danger, to insist on withdrawing. And he was adamant until he was informed that if he refused to ride, he would be suspended. Forced to go against his own instincts, he remounted the temperamental steed and found himself, as the race began, pulling on the reins as hard as he could to keep from being thrown again.

On this day, Murphy was riding for William Cottrill, but it was James Williams' horse Bob Miles who set the pace just ahead of Powhattan III and Audrain, the horse that was favored to win. Meanwhile, Murphy started off far behind in the next to last position. Betty Borries speculates, "Considering the horse's temperament, perhaps the element of survival was even more important to Ike than his first Derby win."[7] And that is how he rode, careful at this point not to demand more of Buchanan than Buchanan was willing to safely give.

Around the first turn and into the backstretch, Admiral took over the lead. Bob Miles fell to second and Loftin took over third. Then Loftin moved into second while Bob Miles continued to fall back until he was in fourth place. By the time they reached the half-mile pole, Admiral held a two-length lead in what was a "killing pace." But then at the three-quarters-of-a-mile pole, that colt essentially quit, falling further and further behind the leaders until suddenly, Buchanan came charging on the outside. Murphy had finally loosened his pull on the horse who, with gigantic strides, took over the lead and quickly stretched it to two lengths. When Murphy won, he had Buchanan under a pull again, to keep the horse from overextending himself. His reputation as the "gentle jockey" intact, he used neither whip nor spur, but guided Buchanan with his arms and hands. No other jockey could have ridden this particular horse so effectively under the circumstances. And perhaps no other trainer but African American William Bird could have prepared this horse in the first place for the strategic surge effected by the jockey.

During the 1884 season, Murphy rode Buchanan in many other races, including the Clark Handicap, also at Churchill Downs. In all, the jockey had 132 mounts that year, winning almost one out of every four in which he had entered. Yet the incident that displayed Murphy's character, more than any racing victory ever could, occurred less than a month after the Kentucky Derby at a race in St. Louis when a horse named Fishburn cut in front of Murphy, causing him and his mount, Bonnie Australian, to go down. That was dangerous enough, but the situation became even more perilous because just as he and Bonnie Australian went down so did yet another horse, Revoke, seriously injuring his rider in the process. Unable to move, Revoke's rider just laid on the track. Thinking quickly, while struggling himself to get out of harm's way, Murphy reached for the fallen white jockey and dragged him off the track and under a fence where he waited for help to arrive.

The following year, Murphy again had 132 mounts, winning such races as the Glidelia Stakes, Hindoo Stakes, Phoenix Hotel Stakes, and the Clark Handicap again. And occasionally, he rode the horse Isaac Murphy that had fittingly been named after him. However, in the Kentucky Derby that year, he could only muster a fifth-place finish amidst the furious homestretch charge of Joe Cotton, Berson, and Ten Booker.

The 1886 Derby was steeped in controversy, particularly due to the absence of any bookmakers, who had been out on strike due to the large fees that they would have had to pay to conduct their operations. Several horse owners were quite disgruntled over this turn of events, but one, James Ben Ali Haggin, went so far as to threaten to remove all his horses from the track unless some accommodation was made. By Derby time, 23 bookmakers were on the scene to Haggin's great satisfaction since he was a firm believer in betting on his own horses and especially wanted to bet on the horse Ben Ali, named after Haggin's own son. Ben Ali would indeed go on to win the 1886 Derby by half a length over Blue Wing, the jockeys on both those horses having whipped their steeds for every inch of ground they could get. Murphy placed a respectable fourth out of the field of ten.

It was a joyous occasion for Haggin until, while celebrating his victory, he was informed that one of the track officials had initially responded rather rudely to his demand for bookmakers. The official had remarked, "Who did Haggin think he was? To hell with him anyway."[8] Haggin became so angry, once he learned about the comment, that in the middle of his celebration, he immediately called for his trainer, and by dawn the entire string of Haggin horses was en route back to New York, never to return again. In fact, for the next quarter of a century, with the exception of Michael Dwyer in 1896, Eastern owners of high class three-year-olds withheld their horses from the Kentucky Derby. Such was Haggin's influence among New York racing circles.

Meanwhile, Murphy was having a fabulous year with numerous wins including victories in the St. Louis Fair Oaks and the Gas Companies Stakes, which was also held in St. Louis. Then at Saratoga, he rode the 1885 Kentucky Derby winner, Joe Cotton, to a victory in the First Sweepstakes and then rode Volante to other victories at the same Saratoga meeting. Ironically enough, at New Jersey's Monmouth Park, Murphy got a chance to redeem himself against Ben Ali, the horse that had beaten him in the 1886 Kentucky Derby. It was the Champion Stakes and Murphy had been commissioned to ride aboard Volante, a horse with which he had had extensive experience. As it turns out, Murphy won the race handily, practically coasting in to victory by a convincing four-length margin.

Murphy was in his racing prime, and most of the horse racing fans who got the chance to watch him ride knew full well that they were seeing something special. Horse owner Ed Corrigan proclaimed of the jockey that "he has not a superior, if, indeed, an equal, as a rider, and is the very embodiment of honesty and integrity. The latter quality, combined with his great ability, makes him immensely popular, and his appearance in the saddle is always greeted with applause, and that of a deafening kind when one of his great finishes sends his mount to victory."[9] It was Corrigan who had named one of his own horses "Isaac Murphy," an act that in itself was of some historic portent. Yet in spite of that honor and the racing popularity that he and some of the other jockeys achieved, they could not rise above the social consequences of their skin color. They would never, for example, have been found in the midst of the dignified gentlemen and fashionable ladies in the clubhouses and grandstands at the very tracks where they nonetheless had to compete.

In a biographical newspaper sketch entitled "The Colored Archer," it was asserted that Murphy "mingles very little with his own race and spends his leisure hours in reading and studying."[10] If such was to any significant extent the case, then Murphy may have found himself, after his climb to fame, caught in a virtual no-man's land between, on one hand, a race that was held in such low regard that he could never be fully accepted there and, on the other hand, a race that still regarded him as somehow inferior.

Even L. P. Tarlton, who was Ike's attorney and the owner of Fleetwood Stables, could not help but betray his own racism even in showering praise, declaring, "If there is any person that would not do a dishonest act, or that can be trusted beyond a money value, it is that colored boy, Isaac Murphy. They say every man has his price, but money can't buy that boy."[11] At the time of that statement, Murphy was in his mid-twenties. In defense of Tarlton, it may have been the case that at five-feet-one-inch tall, Murphy and others like him might have seemed to be in a perpetual state of childhood. That may explain the references to Murphy as a boy even though he was well into his adulthood years. What is not, however, explained away so easily is how in that statement Tarlton generalizes about the circumstances of humankind, with particular reference to men, but then even while praising Murphy refuses to accord him the status of a man.

Racing was the venue where Murphy ultimately was to prove his manhood. Under contract now with E. J. "Lucky" Baldwin, the jockey continued his winning ways on tracks from New York to Baltimore, Louisville, Chicago, and Kansas City. But there was trouble brewing on the horizon. Jockeys had to maintain a low riding weight and many of them used weight-reduction techniques that were extremely dangerous. Fred Archer himself had been one who for years "fought overweight, taking long jogs daily, heavily swathed in sweaters; taking hot baths nightly during the racing season; and dining on champagne and a biscuit."[12] To aid his cause, that English rider furthermore used certain drugs that, combined with his extreme diet and exercise, left him not only physically drained but also severely depressed. Having depleted his immune system to the point where he eventually contracted typhoid fever, he could take it no longer and, on November 8, 1886, committed suicide, shooting himself to death.

As tragic as Archer's death was, it was also an omen of things to come in terms of the direction in which Murphy's own career was headed. In

1887, the jockey won numerous stakes races aboard the Emperor of Norfolk but then, on one occasion, did not do as well as some had expected, whereupon the charge was made that he did not ride as effectively as he might have because he was riding drunk, under the influence of champagne. The allegation, however, was never proven and Murphy went on to have another great year as now the highest paid jockey in the racing industry.

As far as the Kentucky Derby was concerned, he experienced something of a dry spell, finishing last in 1887 and not even riding in 1888. 1889, however, would be different as he finished a respectable third that year aboard Milton Young's Once Again. In all, he had an astounding 195 mounts that year, winning 58 times.

The following year would prove to be both a high point as well as one of the lowest points in his life and career. The track was muddy for the 1890 Derby, the first time a Derby had been rain-soaked. But Murphy stuck to his proven style, falling back into the last position among the six starters just as the race was getting underway. Then, around the first turn and into the backstretch, he moved to the outside and quickly took the lead, gaining a two-length advantage. All at once, every other jockey began whipping his horse as hard as he could, trying to catch the leader. W. R. Letcher's horse, Bill Letcher, seemed to have a chance as he was actually gaining on the Ed Corrigan-owned Riley. But then Murphy loosened his reins a bit and urged Riley back into a two-length lead that he was able to maintain up to the wire. Just as had been the case with his 1884 Derby victory, Murphy never used his whip or spurs, but relied instead on the uncanny ability to know just how fast a horse could go without exhausting himself to the point where he could not effectively contend with any challengers at the end. In this race as in so many others, the strategy worked to absolute perfection.

The act of pulling back on the reins until the appropriate moment in a race may have been more taxing for Murphy than it was for the horses he rode. Immediately after his 1890 Derby win, it was observed that "as Murphy rode back to the judges' stand, he was ... covered with mud all over his body, and his horse fared no better, though not appearing half so much exhausted as his rider. Riley looked not in the least worn out."[13] Though it was certainly not unusual for a jockey to be exhausted at the end of a highly competitive race, there was nonetheless cause to wonder how Murphy could be so thoroughly spent when Riley himself was observed to have been easily able to continue, if he had to, for at least another half-mile at the same pace with which he had won.

Just nine weeks before that second Derby win, Murphy had weighed more than 133 pounds, but by race time he was down to 118. It had become routine for the jockey to balloon out of shape during the winter months and then quickly lose weight in preparation for the riding season. Suspicions about how Murphy accomplished this became more and more centered around the prospect that as he got older he did deprive himself of regular nourishment and resorted to drinking champagne as an alternative to meals.

Disaster struck on August 26, 1890, at Monmouth Park when he was scheduled to ride in the Monmouth Handicap aboard James B. Haggin's horse Firenzi, the odds-on favorite to win. Those high expectations would, however, be dashed, and the humiliating scene was reported in the *New York Times*:

> Murphy's pitiful attempts to ride Firenzi culminated just after the mare passed the judges' stand last when she should have been first. He could not keep her straight, and she bolted over to the inner fence. Murphy had strength enough left to prevent a collision. That was all. As soon as he had practically stopped her, what strength he had was gone and he fell out of the saddle in a heap on the track.[14]

It was not the same situation as had been the case with the recalcitrant Buchanan in 1884, when Murphy was able to finally bring that horse under control and then go on to claim the victory. This time, however, the jockey would lose miserably, never having gotten control of the horse or, for that matter, his own depleted body.

There were many who rushed to the jockey's defense, declaring that he looked in fine condition just moments before the race. A waiter and cashier at the track cafe remembered that he and his wife, who was in attendance for the event, drank only Apollinaris mineral water. Murphy's contention was that he may have somehow been poisoned. The Clerk of Scales insisted that before the race, he was "perfectly sober." After the race, however, he was in so much pain that toward the end of the year, he remained under a doctor's care for what appeared to be an inflamed stomach. During that period, though only 29 years old, he was becoming "haggard and aged," with a face that was becoming increasingly "pinched and drawn."

The *New York Times* made much of the fact that just a few days before the race, Murphy had been present at a festive clambake on the grounds of trainer Matt Byrnes' estate near Eatontown, New Jersey. Politicians and other dignitaries of every level were there and the champagne flowed freely. The guest of honor was Murphy himself who was presented with a silver-mounted whip mainly for the numerous wins he had gotten while

Isaac Murphy and associates at a clambake (courtesy of the Keeneland Library).

riding Salvator, who had garnered a group of men, who called themselves the Salvator Club, a substantial sum of money. The troubling question is just how much, if anything, did Murphy drink? And if he did drink, could the amount of his intake have had such a lingering effect so as to later result in the Monmouth Handicap debacle?

It stands to reason that the Monmouth incident occurred due to a combination of things, including the dangerous dieting regimen which left Murphy weakened on many occasions. His dependence on champagne as a replacement for food must certainly have left him with many of the symptoms of alcoholism, in which case any drinking he might have done at the clambake could have exacerbated his already weakened condition, leaving him further decimated as he had had to quickly shed pounds to meet the weight requirement. The fact that he seemed "perfectly sober" to some people just before the race may not have explained what his condition really was.

Whatever the truth was regarding that loss at Monmouth, it is perhaps most significant that in all of 1890, Murphy raced only 38 times. He won 13 of those events, but at the same time may well have understood that his skills were in a decline. Yet he would recover enough, from whatever caused his ailment, to resume his place among the racing greats of his time.

As a result of Monmouth, Murphy was slapped with a suspension which was another reason for his limited riding, but in 1891, he resumed his career with a vengeance, winning 32 out of the 114 races in which he rode. The Kentucky Derby that year proved to be an intriguing race because in spite of the track being in excellent condition, the race itself wound up being the slowest in Derby history. Kingman's black trainer, Dudley Allen, who was also half owner of that horse, had told Murphy to let Monk Overton on Balgowan get out in front and set the pace. But when the flag was dropped to begin the race, Bashford Manor's Hart Wallace took the lead, followed by High Tariff and then Balgowan and Kingman. Yet none of those four horses ran much faster than a canter for the first full mile and a quarter, the other owners and trainers having evidently issued the same instructions to their jockeys as Allen had given to Murphy. During most of that mile-and-a-quarter distance, Murphy and Overton were content to lay back a short distance to watch one another and let the other two horses have a slight lead.

Charles E. Van Loan's fictional Moseby Jones hoisted in celebration after a victory (drawing by F. C. Yohn for *Collier's*, 1916).

The *Journal-Courier* described it as a "funeral procession" and the crowd of 25,000 was wondering if anything resembling a horse race was ever going to take place at all. Before the event had begun, the throng had swelled to the point where Jim Ferguson, the official starter for the race, was only able to get to the starting line with the help of a police escort who cleared a path for him. Now all of those spectators were becoming disappointed that instead of a contest of speed and endurance, they were watching a cat-and-mouse game.

Then, with a bolt, Overton charged Balgowan out away from the pack in a desperate attempt to reach the finish line first. That was what Murphy had been waiting for all along and he set out to catch the new leader. Into the homestretch, Balgowan led by half a length but Murphy was coming up fast, riding Kingman hard for a one-length lead, which he held to the finish line.

The following year Murphy rode only 42 times and in 1893, the number dropped to 30. Although only 32 years old, his health was failing miserably. In addition to the now more frequent accusations that he was substituting alcohol for food, it was also suspected that he engaged in "flipping," that is, depriving himself of food and then gorging and vomiting it back up, all for the purpose of weight control. He was in all likelihood a chronic bulimic, and in an era before the implications of that disease were even fully understood.

For Murphy, it was simply a matter of getting into the proper condition to ride. Of those 30 mounts in 1893, one would be his last Kentucky Derby ride. The crowd was larger than ever—30,000 in all—but this time it would be jockey Ed Kunze on Lookout who came home the winner without the use of whip or spur, finishing with a comfortable five-length lead. In all, Murphy had ridden in 11 Kentucky Derbies over the course of 17 years, more than any other jockey until Eddie Arcaro broke the record and rode in a total of 21 Derbies in 27 years, from 1935 to 1961.

Murphy had only seven mounts in 1894, and then 20 in 1895, his last year of riding. That year, he won only twice, his last ride a winner aboard Tupto at a fall meeting in Lexington. Several months later, on February 12, 1896, the great jockey died from complications associated with pneumonia. In actuality, his body had become so weakened from the years of debilitating dieting that he could not muster the strength to fend off that final illness.

His funeral was one of the largest in Lexington's history, with over 500 present, including dignitaries and ordinary citizens who braved a cold winter snow to pay their respects to one of the greatest, if not *the* greatest jockey in racing history. At the time of his death, his yearly income was reported to have been nearly $20,000, and according to most estimates he left his wife an estate in the vicinity of $30,000. Still, by most accounts she was relatively poor when she died and had to be buried in what some considered a potter's field that was in actuality the same "Old No. 2" cemetery where her husband had been interred 14 years earlier.

In 1896, a wooden stake was used to mark the place where Murphy was buried. But then in 1909, some prominent horsemen replaced it with a concrete marker that was cast right there where the jockey was buried and then fixed in place. It proved to be an important substitute as in the late 1950s a search was conducted to locate the grave and even with that concrete marker, the search carried on for three years. In 1967, Murphy's bones were exhumed from the "Old No. 2" cemetery and reinterred near the great racehorse Man o' War, who in 1920 had beaten Sir Barton, the 1919 Triple Crown winner, by an astounding seven lengths in a mile-and-a-quarter match race. The new burial site was at Man o' War Memorial Park, one and a half miles west of Lexington. Eddie Arcaro was the honorary chairman of the dedication ceremony.

Murphy's remains would be transferred yet again in the late 1970s and reinterred in the Kentucky Horse Park, north of Lexington. Man o' War was moved along with him. There they both lay in all their majesty, perhaps the greatest jockey of all time and perhaps the greatest horse, at peace in the luxuriant bluegrass hills.

CHAPTER IX

ALONZO CLAYTON
May 11, 1892

Born in 1876, in Kansas City, Missouri, Alonzo Clayton would advance through the jockey ranks and go on to compile, during the years from 1892 to 1897, one of the more outstanding records in Derby history. His career had begun in 1888 when he took a job as an exercise rider for "Lucky" Baldwin in Chicago. The job was originally only supposed to last for a summer, but Clayton remained in Baldwin's employ for nearly a year before he moved on to Clifton, New Jersey, where he then worked for D. A. Honig. By the time Clayton was 13 years old, he was no longer just an exercise boy but now he was racing the horses himself, bringing home his first winner in 1890 at the track in Clifton.

The 1892 Derby was historic for two reasons. First, when Clayton won the Derby that year, he became the youngest person ever to accomplish that feat. Second, the field consisted of only three horses. It was the smallest field in Derby history, a situation that would not occur again until 1905 when steel magnate S. S. Brown's horse Agile would win with jockey Jack Martin aboard, going against Lucien Lyne and Dale Austin on Ram's Horn and Layson respectively.

In 1892, the race at first looked to be a four-horse affair between just two owners. Ed Corrigan had two entries, Huron and Phil Dwyer. George J. Long had entered Azra, who had a praiseworthy 1891 season, winning the Champagne Stakes, placing second in the Essex Stakes, and third in several other significant races. Furthermore, Long had intended to enter Bashford, another proven winner. Such, however, was not to be the case as Long and his trainer, John H. Morris, decided to scratch Bashford because the track had been deemed in poor condition following a downpour.

Yet another horse, Irish Chief, was rumored to be an entry in the field, but when the horses went onto the track to race in that Derby of 1892, Irish Chief was not among the entries. As it turns out, the announcement that he would be running was a ploy on the part of the Louisville Jockey Club to draw as large a crowd as possible to an event that the *Courier-Journal* would later describe as having a "universal feeling of refrigerated disgust." That newspaper went on to say, "It looked to be a poor race. The prediction that Bashford would be drawn was fulfilled early in the day.... There was nothing to inspire enthusiasm. The saddling paddock was empty."[1]

Alonzo Clayton (courtesy of the Keeneland Library).

Owners Long and Corrigan both chose not to parade their horses in front of the grandstand, opting instead to keep them in the stable for as long as possible, perhaps because the weather was still somewhat chilly. In addition to the small field of horses, the weather was also a factor in the relatively small size of the crowd. A year earlier, the Derby had attracted 25,000 spectators. This year, that number fell to only about 10,000.

Corrigan's strategy was simple, that is, at least in theory. Thomas Britton aboard Huron was to set a blistering pace, wear down Azra and thereby allow Monk Overton on Phil Dwyer to win. It was a laudable plan. Charles Parmer, in *For Gold and Glory*, notes that "'Monk' Overton, a Negro rider ... was a favorite in the South and the Midwest during the 'eighties and 'nineties, as popular perhaps as the great Isaac

Murphy."[2] Overton was another gifted rider. At Washington Park in Chicago, on July 10, 1891, he rode six winners out of six mounts on a seven-race card. In the second of those seven races he had no mount at all, or what he accomplished that day might have been even more astounding. Now, in the Derby, Overton should have been Clayton's primary competitor since the plan was not for Britton to win but just wear down Clayton's horse, Azra, so that Overton could then take over the race.

At the beginning of the contest, it must have seemed a blowout was about to occur. Britton on Huron burst into the lead and at the first turn was ahead of Azra by five lengths. Meanwhile, Overton on Phil Dwyer was in last place, a length and a half behind Azra. Clayton knew that he had to be careful in this situation, maintain his composure, and this he did. In assessing the race at this point, the *Courier-Journal* reported, "Under Clayton's good guidance, Azra is holding his own, though seemingly between two fires, for if Huron does not run away from him, there behind him is Phil Dwyer running under a pull and ready to take up the fight."[3] It was in fact like being caught "between two fires," for while Huron seemed to be threatening to break away from the other two horses for good, Overton was waiting for Azra to tire, whereupon he would then ease past both Azra and Huron and on into the lead.

However, that strategy would prove not to be so simple. As the three horses approached the first turn, Huron and Phil Dwyer took to the outside so as to avoid the wettest part of the track. Clayton, on the other hand, was driving Azra toward the inside and although it was the wettest part of the track, Clayton's great skill enabled him to make up valuable ground on the leader so that coming out of the turn, Huron's lead had been reduced to a mere two lengths. Still, Corrigan's jockeys carried on gamely with their original pre-race strategy. Britton pushed Huron on to regain some of the ground he had lost, until the lead had gotten back to three lengths. Meanwhile, Overton had pulled Phil Dwyer up almost even with Azra and prepared to take over second place. But the race would turn out to be not so much between Overton's horse and Clayton's, because just as Britton tried to pull further away in his role as the "rabbit," Clayton was not too far behind while Overton was now having trouble keeping up with both of them as the battle was becoming a head-to-head struggle between Clayton and Britton.

Coming out of the final turn, Azra was still a half-length behind Huron but gaining with every stride until the two horses were neck and neck driving toward the finish. First, Huron had the lead, then Azra took over, and it went back and forth this way for awhile, neither rider able to get his horse more than a nose ahead of the other. By this point, Britton had Clayton pinned on the inside, so close in fact that the latter jockey could not have raised his whip to urge Azra on if he had wanted to do so. Yet neither was Britton using his whip to press Huron toward the wire. The added motion that the whip required would have taken away from the tremendous arm and hand effort that both riders were exerting in their desperation to gain even the slightest advantage. At the wire, it was Clayton on Azra, winning by just a nose.

After the race was over, Overton explained to reporters that the reason he had not "brought up" Phil Dwyer to win towards the end of the race was because he did not feel he needed to. According to the pre-race strategy, Phil Dwyer was to assume the lead once Huron had finished tiring Azra out. But since Huron still had the lead so close to the end, Huron might as well just bring in the victory himself, was how the defeated Overton reasoned it. The reality was that he could not have caught the two leaders if he had wanted to. In fact, he had already lost the race in the backstretch when he summoned Phil Dwyer to catch up with the leaders, and Phil Dwyer just was not able to respond.

Thomas Britton insisted that he thought he had won the race, not an unusual response after such a close finish, but then he quite willingly deferred to the judges as having been in the best position to know. The jockeys were all African American and knew each other well, so in private there was even more banter back and forth about who really won, each being well acquainted with the others' riding prowess.

As the victor, Clayton could afford to be somewhat modest, praising Huron's competitiveness more than praising himself. But they all could be especially proud of the impact they had on what was supposed to have been one of the poorest showings in Derby history. In fact, the exact opposite had occurred. The day after the race, the headlines read, "Smallest Field and Grandest Contest in the History of the Classic Race."[4] In spite of Bashford being scratched from the race and the weather being damp and chilly, the crowd that day saw what was to be heralded as the greatest Derby of all time.

Later that same year, Azra died suddenly. After his Derby victory, he had won the Clark Stakes at Louisville and the Travers Stakes at Saratoga as well as having placed in numerous other races. Then one day, Azra's trainer, John Morris, invited some of his friends to the barn where Azra was being kept. Morris even paraded the prize horse for all of those guests to admire. Once Azra was back in his stall and the guests were elsewhere on the premises, a groom rushed up to Morris to inform him that Azra had fallen down. Upon inspection it was determined that the great racing specimen was dead though only three years old.

Fate would also not bode kindly for Thomas Britton, who had sustained a bad fall while racing at Washington Park in Chicago just one year prior to his spectacular duel with Clayton in the 1892 Kentucky Derby. His performance in the Derby looms as having been all the more incredible as one considers the mental and physical toll that fall had on him. There were even occasions, after the fall, when he would try to talk and the words that he spoke would be totally incoherent.

Yet he continued to race. In 1891, he rode Valera to victory in the Tennessee Derby, and that same year, he won the Kentucky Oaks aboard Miss Hawkins. The following year, the same year that he placed second in the Kentucky Derby, he won the Tennessee Derby again and also rode to victory in the Clipsetta Stakes in Latonia, Kentucky. In 1896, he won five of six events on the racing schedule at an August meeting in Newport, Kentucky. But then, while racing again at Washington Park, he suffered another fall and died shortly thereafter as a result of the injuries that he sustained.

Clayton himself would go on to compete in three more Kentucky Derbies; he would place second twice, and third on one other occasion. The very next year after his 1892 Derby victory, he rode again in the event. As had been the case in his first Derby race, the track was wet, it having rained all day and night before the following day's competition. As it turned out, the horse Lookout had even more experience on wet tracks than Plutus, the horse Clayton rode, and the former wound up winning by a substantial margin.

Two years later, Clayton would again ride in the Derby and find himself pitted once again against Monk Overton as well as a relatively new jockey on the scene, James "Soup" Perkins. The track conditions were perfect, and Clayton was able to place ahead of Overton. But it was Perkins who won the race. It was in effect like the passing of the baton from one rider to another in terms of one particular factor. Clayton, at age 15 in 1892, had been the youngest jockey ever to win the Kentucky Derby. Now he shared the distinction with Perkins who in this year, 1895, had been only 15 years old when he won.

Clayton's final Kentucky Derby run came in 1897. As had been the case in his first two Derby competitions, the track was wet and though Clayton on Ornament was the decided favorite, Typhoon II would provide some stiff competition. The race was very close, but in the end it would be Typhoon II who came in across the finish line first, with Ornament coming in second. Clayton had missed, by just a head, being a two-time Kentucky Derby winner.

Afterwards, Clayton raced for a few more years, winning events such as the Latonia Oaks aboard Sardonic and the California Handicap on Traverser, both races held in 1898. He had won the Clark Handicap in 1892 and 1897, and the Kentucky Oaks in 1894 and 1895. In 1894, he won the Great Western Handicap at Washington Park, and in 1895, he captured the Tennessee Oaks, the Flash Stakes and the United States Hotel Stakes, the latter two races held at Saratoga.

Though he did not win aboard Ornament in the 1897 Kentucky Derby, that same year he did win while riding Ornament in the Latonia Derby. Indeed, he rode that horse to numerous other victories. The 1890s would be the last full decade during which blacks would dominate the field of thoroughbred horseracing. And during that decade, Clayton was among the very best of those African Americans still riding. In the 1893 fall meeting at Churchill Downs, he won the jockey crown, an award given to the rider with the most victories over the course of the events held at that meeting. Three years later, he would compete in the Preakness, one of only three black jockeys ever to do so in that leg of what would come to be known as horseracing's vaunted Triple Crown. He placed third there, but went on to win the St. Louis Derby in 1897 and the Suburban Handicap at Sheepshead Bay in 1898, even as his career in high stakes racing was drawing to a close.

CHAPTER X

JAMES PERKINS
May 6, 1895

Born in Kansas City, Missouri, in 1880, James Perkins began his jockey training when he was 10 years old. By age 11, he was already winning important races and by age 13 he had become one of the dominant riders on the horseracing circuit. In 1893, he was aboard five of the six horses that won on a racing card in Lexington, Kentucky, and that caught the attention of the owners of Fleischmann Stables, where he began riding for a base salary of $4,000 a year in addition to a percentage take from his winning races and any fees he might collect from outside mounts whenever his stable was not racing. He repeated the feat of winning five out of six races on a single card in 1894 at Saratoga, having become something of an heir apparent to Isaac Murphy, who would retire the following year after a career that had established him as perhaps the greatest jockey in history.

Perkins' success in 1894 is all the more remarkable when one considers that he suffered a dangerous fall in October 1893, causing some speculation that he might have lost his courage as a result of that experience. As one reporter recounted the incident, "Jockey 'Soup' Perkins who rode with so much success at the meeting here in Lexington, got a hard fall at Nashville last Tuesday, his mount Merry Eyes going down with him. Perkins was badly stunned and was unconscious for several hours, but the physician who attended him says that he is not injured internally. This is the first fall that Perkins ever got, as far as recalled now, and it may have the effect of making him timid."[1]

The fall, however, did not cause a lapse in courage as was evidenced by his showing the very next year at Saratoga. And he would continue to ride in high stakes events for many years to come, on through the 1902-03 winter season. Eight years after his retirement, he had a heart attack and died while in attendance for a race in Hamilton, Ontario.

Perhaps more telling than the fall from his horse was the regimen of "flipping" that he, like Murphy, was regularly engaged in, requiring him to eat and then purge so as to get his weight down as low as possible for particular races. Though he only needed to get to 122 pounds for the 1895 Derby, on other occasions he was able, through what were actually bouts of bulimia, to reduce his weight all the way down to 88 pounds, the optimum weight for riding two-year-old horses. Murphy drank champagne to keep his energy level up while depriving his body of the calories and nutrition he would have needed to keep himself healthy. Soup must have served the same purpose for Perkins. In fact, that light meal became such a staple in his diet that it eventually became part of his name as he soon became known as "Little Soup" or, somewhat more formally, James "Soup" Perkins.

James "Soup" Perkins (courtesy of the Keeneland Library).

The year of 1895 was the year that the United States Supreme Court ruled, in the case of *Gibson v. Mississippi*, that blacks had not been excluded from jury duty merely on the basis of their race. The ridiculousness of that holding is most starkly realized upon considering that 7,000 of the 8,500 men declared competent for jury duty, in just one of the Mississippi counties, were black and not one of them got the chance to sit in a jury box. Such were the times in the South and such was the nature of the Supreme Court itself to allow infringement on certain freedoms when it came to African Americans.

Yet black jockeys still dominated horseracing in the South. Among

Perkins' competitors in the 1895 Derby were Alonzo Clayton, who had won three years earlier, and Monk Overton, who some experts felt was just as good as Isaac Murphy. In all, there were only four entrees in the Derby that year, perhaps owing as much as anything else to the uncertainty that surrounded the Churchill Downs racetrack's future. As of 1895, the track had not been a profitable venture. Business was so bad that the Downs' directors ordered it sold in 1894, and a new group took over stewardship. One of the first things that the new owners did was provide the Downs with a physical layout for what it actually looks like today. Matt Winn describes the ownership change and the ensuing new construction in terms of a passing of the torch from the man who began the Derby, M. Lewis Clark, to a new breed of entrepreneurs:

> The new owners of the Downs pooled $100,000 and decided to make some revolutionary changes. The old grandstand, as well as Clark's clubhouse were torn down, and barns replaced them on that site. Then work was started on the construction of the grandstand on the opposite side of the track, where patrons would be free from the glare of the afternoon sun.
> That grandstand, 285 feet long at the time, is the same stand, with its outlines marked by the two weather-whipped steeples, towering into Kentucky skies, which marks almost dead center of the combined clubhouse-grandstand structure at Churchill Downs today.[2]

In spite of the changes to the physical structure of the Downs, the 1895 Derby was by most accounts not successful. Some of this had to do with the race's one-and-a-half-mile distance. It was now becoming generally understood that this was too great a distance to ask a three-year-old horse to run at full speed so early in the year. But it would be one more year before the race's length would be reduced by a quarter mile.

Perkins aboard Halma was the overwhelming favorite to win the race. As a two-year-old, he won two of the seven races that he was entered in back East, and he placed in several other events. Byron McClelland had purchased him as a yearling from the Eastin and Larrabie Farm near Lexington and trained him through his two-year-old season and on into the next year where he continued to show great promise. His victory at the Phoenix Hotel Stakes at Lexington, just before the Derby, led to generally high expectations.

McClelland and Perkins must have known just how special Halma was because at the very beginning of the race that jockey had wrapped the horse's reins around his arms all the way up to his elbows, not even worried apparently that by holding him back so he might lose substantial ground. Perkins knew what he was doing, though, because in spite of holding Halma back, the horse tore into the lead anyway, with Clayton and Overton slightly behind in the second and third positions, on Laureate and Curator respectively. Willie Martin, riding Basso, was bringing up the rear.

Commenting after the race was over, Martin explained that once the race had begun, he never thought it was possible to win. So he was more concerned about how he could at least beat Laureate and Curator. Said Martin, "Halma could have taken 140 pounds and easily beaten the field against him to-day. He had the race won before he had gone the first quarter, because he had by that time showed how he outclassed his company."[3] It was quite a claim to make, that Halma could have carried an additional 20 pounds in weight and still won the Derby easily.

But Martin's comment was not so outlandish as one might think. Passing the grandstand the first time, Halma was already leading by a length and steadily increasing that lead as Perkins, with his arms still wrapped up to the elbows with the reins, was actually holding the horse in check. Perkins himself would later describe:

> I had an easy thing of it. I never let go Halma's head.... I had to hold him clear to the finish. There was no place in the race when I could not have gone away from the field as I pleased, and I felt safe. Halma could have gone six miles further and beat such horses as those.... All I had to do was to sit still and hold him.[4]

One jockey said that Halma could have carried an extra 20 pounds and still won. The winning jockey insisting that if the race had been six miles longer, Halma still would have won. Such was the extent to which Halma overwhelmed the rest of the field. The *Courier-Journal* reported that at the one-mile pole, Perkins was "motionless" and Halma looked like he was exerting no more energy than what he would in an "easy exercise cantor." Halma would eventually win by five lengths, a distance that observers contended could have easily been 20 lengths if that was what Perkins had wanted. Indeed, at the end of the race, Perkins still had the reins wrapped all the way up to his elbows. He had been holding Halma back the whole time.

Early in the race, Clayton's saddle split wide open, but he acknowledged that even if his saddle had remained intact, he would not have been able to beat Perkins. Overton, after the race, conveyed utter exasperation, explaining how way before the race's end his horse, Curator, had essentially quit running, leaving him no choice but to apply the whip in an effort to get him going again. Like Clayton and Martin, though, Overton conceded that he never had a chance to beat Halma, who could have "run all over" the rest of the field if he had wanted to.

After the Derby, Perkins continued to excel on the racetrack, winning, among the more prestigious races, the St. Louis Derby and Tennessee Oaks in 1896. Once his riding career had ended just after the turn of the twentieth century, he became a successful trainer, not as prominent as his brother William but then again, William, although he tried, would never become the same quality jockey that his Derby-winning brother had been. James would later die at the age of 31, even younger than Murphy was when he died, both men having essentially killed themselves to be among the best in their profession.

CHAPTER XI

WILLIE SIMMS
May 6, 1896; May 4, 1898

In 1868, under the auspices of federal Reconstruction mandates, 32 African Americans were elected into the Georgia legislature, and then were summarily expelled when the white members of that political body voted 83 to 23 (the black legislators were not allowed to vote) to deny them eligibility. The rationale for expulsion was that the "Georgia constitution of 1868 failed to specifically grant black men the right to hold public office in Georgia."[1] Those black politicians were later reinstated but not without a struggle and continued animosity from whites who still believed that being a state representative was not an appropriate occupation for blacks. Such was the racial climate in Georgia just after the Civil War.

What happened in that legislature was a reflection of even more extensive horrors that African Americans had to suffer. The Freedmen's Bureau in Georgia

> reported incidents of violence in at least fifty-nine different counties that undoubtedly represented only a small number of the actual incidents that occurred. Most abuses went unreported. It is impossible to determine the true number of victims who experienced death, beatings, threats, economic pressure, and other forms of intimidation.... Henry Turner, one of the expelled legislators, testified before the 1871 congressional committee investigating the Klan that between fifteen and sixteen hundred blacks had been murdered in Georgia.[2]

Born on the outskirts of Augusta, Georgia, on January 16, 1870, Willie Simms was well aware of the racial circumstances that impacted on the lives of so many blacks in his native state. Having developed a love for horses, he learned as much as he could and then used his equine expertise riding for various owners until he finally made his way to the North. Among the luminaries for whom he rode was Congressman William Scott, who at first had little faith in Simms until the jockey began winning races even though the horses he rode were the decided underdogs. And for a time, Simms still only got "duds" to ride, still nonetheless pulling out victories where they were least expected.

Then in 1891, owner Philip Dwyer engaged Simms as a rider, and a long string of victories was established to the point where by 1893 Simms was considered the best jockey in America. Riding Promenade, he won the Spinaway Stakes in 1891. Then in 1892, he won the Flatbush Stakes on Lady Violet, the Tidal Stakes on Charade, and the First and Second Special races, both while riding Lamplighter. The following year, he rode Comanche to victory in the Belmont Stakes, a performance that he would repeat in 1894, riding Henry of Navarre. This same year, he once again won the First and Second Specials plus the Dwyer Stakes, the Juvenile Stakes, the Swift Stakes, the Tidal Stakes, and the Lawrence Realization, a race he had also won previously in 1893.

Heading into 1895, Simms was still America's leading jockey. By this time, Michael Dwyer had broken partnership ties with his brother Philip and embarked for England to undertake new horseracing ventures. In this endeavor Michael engaged Simms, who not only continued his winning record but also introduced a new riding style that consisted of him leaning far forward in the saddle, crouched over the horse's neck and shoulders, his feet tucked into stirrups that were significantly shorter than what was typical for the English rider. And the English were appalled. They had been so used to riding while sitting upright in the saddle with long stirrups, that they sarcastically referred to Simms' display as him being a "monkey on a stick" and they proclaimed that "monkeyship has supplanted jockeyship."

The *Courier-Journal*, in commenting on the new partnership between Michael Dwyer and Richard Croker, described the results of their employment of Simms:

> Last year Sims [sic] was taken to England, when Dwyer and Croker made their pilgrimage to twist the Lion's tail, and every one knows how much attention his peculiar style of riding attracted over there. The cockneys did not like 'is "feet" or 'is 'ands or 'is 'ead, but Willie showed

them a few things ... that made the haughty Britishers turn crimson in spots, and they very soon found out that they had best cease their criticism of his methods until they could find some native rider who could do better.[3]

That was what the Louisville newspaper had to say about Simms the day after he won the 1896 Derby, giving him credit for being "one of the crack jockeys in the country." And on his foray into English racing, he had likewise established his dominance. "The country" that the newspaper had reference to was indeed America, but just one year before his Derby win, Simms had also accumulated enough victories in England to make him one of that country's leading riders also.

While the *Courier-Journal* acknowledged that Simms had introduced a new, more effective

Willie Simms (*Munsey's Magazine*, 1900).

riding style to the English turf, others were anxious to deny him that particular distinction, wishing instead to say that it had been Indiana-born Tod Sloan who introduced the high-in-the-saddle riding style to England. Writing in the December 1900 issue of *Munsey's Magazine*, Elisha Warfield Kelly declared that "Sloan is probably the greatest jockey that ever lived."[4] That commentator further stated that "in the middle of September, Sloan was retained by the Prince of Wales.... His engagement by the prince means an absolute surrender of English beliefs, and an acknowledgment that American methods are the best."[5] The "American methods" to which Kelly referred were the equivalent of the riding style that Simms had introduced two years before Sloan had even arrived in England. Quite possibly, it was Sloan's high profile as a jockey for the Prince of Wales that enabled him to be more emulated than Simms and thus more often credited for having introduced the high-riding style to England. But racism was at least as crucial a factor in English jockeys and other observers such as Kelly ignoring the importance of Simms' contribution.

Kelly's article, entitled "Our Horses and Jockeys Abroad," was a rather prideful report on America's involvement with English horseracing in general. The author went to great lengths to make the argument that Sloan was the greatest jockey in the world. But that author also provided biographies for other American jockeys who were plying their trade on the Continent. In addition to Sloan, Kelly chronicled the career of Henry "Skeets" Martin from Titusville, Pennsylvania, and "the Reiff boys," Johnny and Lester, from Kokomo, Indiana. Kelly even included a table that specified the various jockeys' total number of mounts, number of victories, and their individual winning percentages. No such detailed information was included for Simms, no biographical data except (almost as if to contradict the article itself) a caption under a photograph of Simms that read, "Willie Sims [sic], who was the first American jockey to ride in England."[6] How could he not be included in some form or fashion, having contributed so profoundly to the American jockey "invasion" of England, bringing with him, as Lynn Renau puts it, the "innovative, aerodynamically balanced" riding style?

A question remains, however, concerning exactly how much credit any of those jockeys (including Simms) should get for their participation on the English turf. It is fascinating that Kelly begins his article with the following momentous proclamation: "Forty five years ago an American horse had never won a race abroad; an American jockey had never ridden in an English race."[7] In other words, at the point of 1855, no American jockeys had ridden there and no American horses had ever won there either. The very next year, however, American owner Richard Ten Broeck took a whole stable of thoroughbreds to England and began winning with those horses to the point where, as Kelly informs, "Mr. Ten Broeck was made much of in London. He was introduced to the Prince of Wales, and became his fast friend."[8] We recall that the Prince of Wales, in later years, will do much to enhance Tod Sloan's career. Needless to say, it was in large part because Ten Broeck and Sloan were white that they were thereby privy to such acquaintances and consequent turf recognition.

But who were the jockeys riding in England for Ten Broeck in 1856? English jockeys? An American horse owner hiring English jockeys all the time? If that were the case, then as victories accumulated, one imagines that the riders would have achieved some degree of fame. Kelly, recounting the victory of a Ten Broeck horse named Prioress, describes, "Her great victory was in the Cesarewitch, a race at two miles, two furlongs, and twenty eight yards. There were thirty seven starters, the very best horses on the English turf."[9] In spite of the significance of that race, Kelly makes no mention of who the winning jockey was. Historian Arthur Ashe reminds us that "in those days the jockeys hardly received much acclaim. The owners were accorded the plaudits."[10] And yet Ashe was also careful to note that as early as just "after the Revolutionary War ... horse owners and trainers realized that the rider, or jockey, was frequently more important than the horse itself."[11] Such knowledge on the part of owners, however, did not stop them from taking credit for the accomplishments of the property that they owned, be it horses or slaves. "By 1800 in the South," as Ashe further explains, "the vast majority of jockeys were diminutive slaves who had grown up around horses all their lives."[12] So, when Ten Broeck ventured over to England in 1856, he may very well have had black slaves riding for him, but in his mind and the minds of the English, their names were insignificant. Among those riders might have been great jockeys whose greatness was never documented: Caesar, Jesse, Scipio, Pompei, and "Crescendo" John among them, those jockeys who might very well have contributed to the development of a riding style and legacy for which they now, due to the lack of a willingness to chronicle it during their lifetimes, may never be adequately recognized.

While acknowledging Simms' contribution in showing this style of riding beyond America's shores, Hotaling argues that the style had its origins at an earlier point in American history:

> The style was inspired by the short, fierce Colonial quarter races, in which crouching and clinging definitely beat getting knocked off the animal. It was employed, too, by American Indians on the horses they acquired from the Spanish. English visitors had noticed it most often on black riders, but the slave-holding congressman John Randolph had used it in his own quarter-racing days, earning him one of the first comparisons of the crouching jock with a monkey on a horse.[13]

The crouching style, contends Hotaling, harkens all the way back to the earliest days of horseracing in America, back as far as the 1700s when white men, referred to as gentleman jockeys, rode their own horses in races, one horse against another horse down a narrow quarter-mile route in the middle of the wilderness. It is not inconceivable that some crouching was done by these taller, bigger men who often had to keep their heads lowered just to avoid tree branches along the racing path. Added to the controversy of who originated the crouching style, is the question of whether a reference to Congressman Randolph as a "monkey on a horse" carried with it the same implications that the term "monkey on a stick" had when applied to the black jockey Simms as he displayed his crouching style before the 1890s English crowds. As Hotaling observes, Sloan would later use the crouching style "and be accused of turning jockeyship into 'monkey-ship.' But he was not covered with racial hatred."[14] No one would declare that either Randolph or Sloan were inferior missing links in an evolutionary chain even if their riding styles did conjure up images of monkeys in the African wild.

Native Americans may have employed the crouching style as well but even they were not as vulnerable to the racial epithets experienced by black jockeys who had raced first as slaves two hundred years before the Civil War and then as free Americans with an even more paradoxical status after that war had ended. When Willie Simms rode Ben Brush to victory in the 1896 Derby, he was not only competing to win what was coming to be recognized as America's pre-eminent horseracing event, but he was also fighting to maintain a recognition of African American excellence in one of the few areas of endeavor in which blacks at least had the semblance of some sort of parity.

This was the same year that the United States Supreme Court, in *Plessy v. Ferguson*, would reinforce a second-class citizenship status for blacks in general as it denied a black train passenger the right to sit where he wished. The reasoning of the Court was that "he has been deprived of no property, since he is not lawfully entitled to the reputation of being a white man."[15] Just three decades after slavery, "white" still meant superior, and "black" was still a virtual brand of inferiority.

The 1896 race was another one of the more exciting Kentucky Derbies up to that time. James Perkins, winner of the Derby the previous year, would be riding Semper Ego for L. B. Ringgold. There would be William Walker, who having won the Derby in 1877, would now be aboard The Winner, owned by William Wallace. Monk Overton, of course black, and Robert Williams, also black, would be riding The Dragon and Ulysses, respectively. Moreover, that latter horse was owned by yet another black man, Edward Brown, who had been a leading jockey himself as a youth in the 1860s, and was now an established trainer and racehorse entrepreneur. A total of 171 horses had been nominated for the race. Eight horses were finally selected from that huge field, and most of the jockeys who rode in the race were African-American.

Kentucky Derby chronicler Matt Winn described the race as "cyclonic." Semper Ego took the early lead with The Winner close behind. Meanwhile, Ben Brush had stumbled badly at the beginning of the race, almost throwing Simms out of his saddle. Many in the crowd of 25,000 spectators watched breathlessly, sensing that the horse was out of the race until,

as the *Courier-Journal* reported, Simms "picks him up at once and begins to place him, lying well in toward the rail in fourth place."[16] Coming around the first turn, First Mate moved into the lead, with The Winner in second place, Semper Ego third, and Ben Brush holding on to fourth. Ben Eder, who would finally come in a close second, was a full twelve lengths behind at the half-mile pole.

As that bunch of four leading horses approached the old grandstand on the side of the track opposite the starting line, Simms moved pass The Winner, pulling even with Semper Ego who was now in second place. Meanwhile, Ben Eder began his surge from far behind to the point where in the homestretch, just one furlong away from the finish line, the race became a vicious battle between the two Bens. It had been Simms' philosophy that "at the finish [of a race] the less a rider uses the whip the better.... A horse is at the end of a journey tired, and all the support you can give him helps his chances."[17] Such was reminiscent of Isaac Murphy's perspective on how to handle his mount, himself having been one who spared the whip and spur, relying instead on his own arm and hand strength.

Simms likewise had tremendous arm and hand strength, having, we will remember, actually pulled Ben Brush out of what looked to be a fateful stumble. But Ben Eder's ferocious burst toward the finish line forced Simms to go against his own advice, using not only his whip but, as Ben Eder charged past him into the lead, Simms

> sinks the steel deep into [Ben Brush's] heaving sides, and as he gives this summons to the colt's innate courage he helps him onward with his hands.... Ben Eder seems a sure winner. But Sims [sic] is still riding and Ben Brush is still fighting. The rowels are rammed still deeper into the gashed sides.... They are even and the wire is overhead. Ben Eder's nose is a bit in front.... And so Sims [sic] makes his final effort.... With hands, heels, head and heart he lifts Ben Brush forward first past the post, with bleeding sides and throbbing flanks.[18]

Ben Eder was arguably the better horse in that race. That son of 1880 Kentucky Derby winner Fonso had had an excellent racing season leading up to the Derby and was thought to be in better overall condition than Ben Brush, although Ben Brush was the official favorite.

It is also of some significance that Ben Brush had been trained by Edward Brown, who as a boy had been nicknamed "Brown Dick" by the earlier black trainer Ansel Williamson. Williamson had so named Brown after the horse, Brown Dick, one of the fastest thoroughbreds in the country at the time. Brown himself had been quite fast, both in terms of his foot speed and in terms of his riding ability. Purchased by the prominent horse breeder Robert A. Alexander at the Lexington, Kentucky, slave market when he was only eight years old, Brown would, by the time he was 16, be one of the two leading jockeys in America. Perhaps his most notable race as a jockey was in 1870 when he rode Kingfisher to victory at the Belmont Stakes. However, it is a sad commentary that reports on that race consistently refer to Brown as only "W. Dick," causing the achievement to almost be lost in history.

Taking full advantage of the knowledge he had gained from Williamson, Brown retired from riding and, by the early 1870s, had become a trainer himself. It was, we will recall, Brown who would wind up training Baden-Baden, the 1877 Derby winner. And it was he who purchased Ben Brush at an 1894 yearling sale and then trained him the following year to numerous stakes victories and several handicap wins as well. Then he sold Ben Brush to Michael Dwyer for a sum variously estimated to have been between $15,000 and $25,000. Though Hardy Campbell was the horse's trainer at the time of his 1896 Derby run, it was Brown who initially spotted the horse in the midst of a herd and then made him into a great racehorse.

Brown did the same with the horse that would become the 1898 Kentucky Derby winner. He purchased and trained Plaudit into stellar racing form before selling him to John E. Madden, who wisely engaged Simms to be the rider. It was in essence the combination of Brown and Simms that was responsible for two Derby victories within the three-year period from 1896 to 1898. The intervening year had likewise been a remarkable one for Simms as, among his more significant victories were the First and Second Specials, the Brighton and Suburban Handicaps, and the Tidal, Tremont, and Withers Stakes, most of those races won on Ben Brush.

Now Simms would be in his second Kentucky Derby. In spite of there having been a record 179 nominations, only four horses were finally entered. The race, however, would still be a tremendous challenge for Simms because the horse who was favored, Lieber Karl, had accumulated an impressive string of victories during the early spring season down in the Memphis area. So sure was one track official of a Lieber Karl victory that he predicted the horse "will run by the others like an express train passes a hand car."[19] Another official declared, "There is nothing in the race but Lieber Karl."[20] And so the stage was set for another dramatic Derby race, another in which Simms would display what the *Courier-Journal* characterized as the "masterly horsemanship of a great rider" in the midst of a tremendous equine battle.

At the beginning of the race, Lieber Karl broke away from the rest of the field, quickly establishing a one-and-a-half-length lead going into the first turn. Coming out of the turn, Lieber Karl continued to hold his comfortable lead as first Han d'Or and then Isabey began falling further and further back in spite of their riders applying all the pressure they could. The race was now between Simms on Plaudit and Tom Burns on Lieber Karl.

As the two leaders reached the half-mile pole, Plaudit was slowly losing ground as Simms settled into a hard but steady riding style, concerned not to push the horse beyond his limit with so much track left yet to cover. That is how it remained as the horses came down the backstretch, with Lieber Karl still pulling away to the point where Simms himself "thought at that time that the race was all over, and Lieber Karl would be the winner."[21] In both of Simms' Kentucky Derby races, there was ill-feeling between him and his nearest competitor, an animosity beyond the simple competitiveness of two determined rivals. Ben Eder's rider, in 1896, had tried to get Simms to say that he lost the race in spite of having been officially declared the winner. That particular race had indeed been so close that there was in all likelihood some room for debate.

Now in 1898, the ill-feeling was even more severe. In fact before the race, the president of Churchill Downs, M. Lewis Clark, threatened both Simms and Burns with a lengthy suspension if either of them violated the code of good sportsmanship. So, in what must have been more than just a race against another jockey, Simms was biding his time, riding like the master horseman he was. Coming out of the final turn, Lieber Karl was still in front, but Simms had now begun pressing Plaudit to go as fast as he could. Lieber Karl still seemed to be running easy while Plaudit was struggling to catch up. It was coming into the homestretch that Simms realized he had a good chance to win. His horse was indeed closing ground but then began to "wobble" under the strain of having been practically pushed to the limit.

This was when, as Simms himself put it, Plaudit began to run "entirely on his courage." The jockey had tried, and successfully so, to keep his horse within striking distance and now just as he was in position to move ahead, he had to "steady him down a little" before he could push hard again. Having accomplished this and with just one eighth of the race to go, it was down to a battle of courage between Lieber Karl and Plaudit and the two men who rode them. Both riders dug in their heels, began whipping brutally, and drove their horses with all the strength they had in their hands. When it was all over, Simms had won his second Kentucky Derby, again by a nose. Plaudit went on to reap a fortune in stud fees for his owner.

Simms, as a consequence of having raced to his second ferocious Kentucky Derby victory, was acknowledged as now the greatest jockey alive.

He would never again race in a Kentucky Derby. However, the same year that he won the Derby for the second time, he also won the Preakness aboard Sly Fox, thus making him the only African American jockey to, at some point or another, win each of the Triple Crown events. He continued riding for only a few more years after that, able to get mounts due in large part to the reputation he had acquired of being "reliable and conservative." After his riding days had ended, he was spotted at the 1909 Derby where he expressed that if he could "make the weight," he would ride again. But by this time he was nearly 40 years old; his words of self-assertion were perhaps made only in jest. His appearance at the 1909 Derby was, as in the case of other African American Derby winners in their later years, the enactment of a ritual, a self-acknowledgment of his incredible contribution, even in the face of a creeping historical forgetfulness of his outstanding accomplishments.

For a while, Simms trained thoroughbreds for flat racing and steeplechase racing, the latter a field to which many black riders turned as opportunities in flat racing disappeared. Simms' high-stirrup riding style proved to be a distinct advantage in the steeplechase racing too. In later years he moved to Asbury Park, New Jersey, to live with his widowed mother, and there he died on February 26, 1927. His body was, however, taken to a farm near Lexington, Kentucky, to be interred in the same state where he had contributed so much to horseracing history.

CHAPTER XII

JAMES WINKFIELD
April 29, 1901; May 3, 1902

As was the case with so many others, James Winkfield began his career as an exercise boy at various Kentucky racetracks. Born on April 12, 1882, he had begun racing by age 15. Ironically, his very first race resulted in catastrophe. Trying to take the lead, he drove for the rail but cut so close across the other three horses that all four horses and riders fell to the ground in a dangerous pile-up. "Wink," as he would come to be known in riding circles, was summarily slapped with a one-year suspension, a quite inauspicious beginning. That early recklessness, though, would evolve into a caginess that served him well in later races and with his life in general.

Two years after that initial mishap, Winkfield found himself riding in the 1900 Kentucky Derby aboard J. C. Cahn's horse, Thrive. This first Derby of the twentieth century had a record number of spectators, 30,000 in all. The favorite was Charles Smith's Lieutenant Gibson, who had won seven of the 18 races he had been in as a two-year-old. On four other occasions he placed second, and twice he came in third. He was the clear-cut favorite to win this 26th installment of the Derby and although he did not break away from the field immediately, by the first turn he was in the lead and would win without his jockey Jimmy Boland even having to make him extend himself. Winkfield placed third in that race, just behind Clyde Van Dusen on Florizar. Van Dusen went on to become a highly

James Winkfield (courtesy of the Keeneland Library).

esteemed trainer and would actually win the 1929 Kentucky Derby with Clyde Van Dusen, a horse named after the trainer himself. Winkfield did not win the 1900 Kentucky Derby race, but he had been beaten by great riders who would become legendary. Boland not only won the 1900 Derby, but did it in a record time that would stand for more than a decade. Such was the level of Winkfield's competition.

The following year, 1901, Winkfield would ride again in the Derby and once again find Jimmy Boland among the competition. Needless to say, Boland was anxious for the shot at a second Derby victory, and a substantial number of spectators were there at the Downs in hopes of watching him accomplish that feat. Boland would be riding Driscoll for owner Woodford Clay, but the horse actually favored to win was Alard Scheck, owned by John W. Schorr of Memphis, Tennessee. So many gamblers were confident that Alard Scheck, with his Scottish-born jockey, would win that

> From a betting standpoint the race was perhaps one of the best in the history of the local track. Alard Scheck was decidedly the favorite with the majority of the public.... Tennessee money flooded the ring for a few minutes and a great deal of local money was placed on Alard Scheck.[1]

Though not to the extent as was the case with Alard Scheck, there was nonetheless a substantial amount of betting on His Eminence, owned by F. B. Van Meter, and to be ridden by Winkfield, both Van Meter and Winkfield hailing from the Lexington area. Most of the betting on Van Meter's horse was done by the Lexington faithful.

In one sense this race was a repeat of the 1898 Kentucky Derby in which Schorr's Tennessee colt Lieber Karl was pitted against another Lexington horse, John E. Madden's Plaudit. Lieber Karl had been the favorite, but Madden's colt wound up winning and keeping the Kentucky Derby crown at home. In 1901, the rivalry between those two states was reinstated with the same result, a Kentucky horse winning over the favorite from Tennessee.

The next day the *Courier-Journal* described how Winkfield had "rated" His Eminence "beautifully," that is did an excellent job of setting a pace with which his horse had the greatest chance to win. Just fifty yards into the race His Eminence was clearly out in front with Alard Scheck and Driscoll close behind. Around the first turn, it was those three horses still out in front with His Eminence slowly pulling away, never to be really challenged for the duration of the race. By the time he reached the three-quarters pole, Winkfield had taken His Eminence out to a three-length lead and had to "shake him up" a bit only near the end when Jimmy Boland and a couple of the other riders began "whipping and digging the rowels" into their horses' sides in a desperate attempt to catch the leader who up to that point, as Winkfield described it, had been just "breezing" right along. Said Winkfield,

> I got him away a little ahead, and after that I just breezed him around the track. Until I entered the stretch I let him go just as easy. All the way I kept a good hold of his head and never moved on him. In the stretch I looked back and saw Sannazarro coming along. I tell you, I shook up His Eminence some then and he came in easy. I think I could have won in faster time if I had wanted to work him, but he had it all his own way, anyhow, so what was the use?[2]

While Winkfield had kept His Eminence out in front for the entire race, he was still concerned not to press him too hard, instead saving something for the homestretch in case it was needed. When Sannazarro, Driscoll, and Amur all began their charge, Winkfield had to apply relatively little pressure on his horse to hit the finish line first, still with a two-length lead. Alard Scheck was so demoralized by His Eminence's dominance of the race that when his jockey tried his best to push him to catch the leader, Alard Scheck "sulked," refusing to be pushed any more, and he ultimately finished in last place, five lengths behind the next to last finisher, Amur.

The year of 1901 was only Winkfield's third full year of riding, and by now his reputation was that of being something of a daredevil at times if he thought that approach would secure him a victory. All the other jockeys in that year's Derby, however, were quick to point out that there had been no interference and that indeed Winkfield had won the race fair and square. It would be just one of 161 races that Winkfield would win in just that year alone.

Winkfield's 1902 Kentucky Derby win would not be quite so easy. The first difficulty he had was in getting the horse that he wanted, and in doing just that, he would have to employ the technique of the African American folkloric character, Br'er Rabbit. Thomas C. McDowell, a great-grandson of Henry Clay, had contracted with white jockey Nash Turner to ride in the race, promising that he could have his choice of mounts. However, the savvy Winkfield was already at the Downs, giving both Alan-a-Dale and The Rival their early morning workouts. McDowell must have been assuming that in the days before the Derby, "Wink" would help him determine which was the faster horse so that that horse could then be given to Turner.

However, Winkfield had already learned which was the faster of the two horses, and in those workouts, he saw it as his task to not show McDowell that Alan-a-Dale was faster, but instead keep that information from the owner who never had his best interests at heart in the first place. In the workouts, Winkfield held Alan-a-Dale back, never allowing him to run his fastest. Meanwhile, in those workouts, he pushed The Rival to go just about as fast as he could. When the times were compared, The Rival seemed to be the superior animal, and so when Turner arrived in town, he naturally chose The Rival to ride, leaving the presumed slower horse, Alan-a-Dale, for Winkfield to ride in the Derby. Two other horses were entered in the race: T. W. Moore's Inventor and the favorite, George C. Bennett's Abe Frank.

As the flag fell, Turner took The Rival out front, but he would not hold the lead for long because Winkfield, with his "good judgment and cold nerve," took over before they reached the first sixteenth pole. Willie Coburn had been instructed to hold Abe Frank back at the beginning and let the others fight it out, and then come on strong once they had substantially expended their energy. Coming out of the first turn, Alan-a-Dale led by two lengths and had extended it to four lengths by the time he reached the quarter-mile pole. Abe Frank and The Rival were a neck apart from each other, vying for the second position. Inventor was now in last place, but just by a half-length behind the other two pursuers of Alan-a-Dale.

As was the case with Coburn, "Tiny" Williams, who was riding Inventor, had been instructed to hold his horse back, it being believed that Alan-a-Dale would be tired out by the first three quarters of a mile and have to quit at that point. Winkfield went out ahead and set the pace, going so fast that he himself felt that Alan-a-Dale might have done the first three fourths of a mile in record-breaking time. As his lead grew to six lengths, Winkfield let up some, knowing that Alan-a-Dale would not be able to hold that pace and would need to have some energy saved for the final stretch.

Winkfield was absolutely right in his thinking that Alan-a-Dale would need to have some energy in reserve because at the top of the homestretch all three of the other horses made their charge. Abe Frank was now within two lengths of the leader and was, in the words of one observer, "coming like the wind." The Rival and Inventor were coming on just as strong, both those horses at Abe Frank's neck, all three about to overtake Alan-a-Dale. It seemed that Winkfield's horse was about to lose, but then for the first time in the race, Winkfield dug his rowels into Alan-a-Dale's sides, lashing him back and forth across the shoulders, calling on the horse to give it all he had.

Although Alan-a-Dale was a very fast horse, he was also reputed to be a "bad-legged" horse who could break down right in the middle of a race. In fact, a great deal of his training had been done with a two-wheeled vehicle called a "sulky" in which the horse had only to pull an exercise boy instead of carrying him on his back. But now a rider was on his back, and as Winkfield kept whipping him to stay ahead, the horse did break down, came up lame right there in the homestretch with the other three horses bearing down on him. Then something striking occurred. Alan-a-Dale kept right on running, nonetheless, as hard as he could while Winkfield worked on figuring out how he might still be able to win in spite of this new dilemma.

One could easily argue that once Winkfield saw that his horse was hurt, he should have brought him to a halt. That would have been humane. However, jockeys understood well what a prestigious win might mean in terms of advancing their livelihoods. Owners also understood the significance in terms of potential wealth and fame. Furthermore, some of the most heralded horses in the racing world were the ones who were willing, quite literally, to run themselves to death for a victory.

With his horse still galloping hard out in front, Winkfield devised a plan that is somewhat reminiscent of what he did in his very first outing just a few years earlier when he cut across the other three horses, causing a pile-up for which he was suspended for a year. In spite of that layoff, he won his very next race although it was only the second of his career. It was almost as if the suspension, and the reason for it, engendered fear in other riders, a fear that in later races would work to their own disadvantage. On top of that, Winkfield was cunning as he himself averred in explaining how he dispatched first Abe Frank and then the others:

When the favorite come up on my shoulder I rode him out into that deep sand; it told on him, and he stopped. The other two horses tried to come inside me, but I ducked back on the rail; when they tried to come around I took them outside, too, both at once. Just a little, you know, enough to get 'em in that sand. And that's all that saved me.[3]

In those days the Churchill Downs track was covered with a thick layer of sand and it would be left there until, in preparation for a race, the ground crew would push it to the outside, making it so the horses that ran the closest to the rail were the ones that had the best footing. When Abe Frank started to pass Alan-a-Dale, Winkfield merely kept that other horse far enough to the outside so that the sand became too much of a problem for Coburn to overcome.

While Winkfield was so engaged, Williams and Turner saw an opening and tried to make a move on the inside. But Winkfield moved back over just in time to cut them off. Inventor and The Rival had had enough strength left to wage a valiant battle against Alan-a-Dale and, in all likelihood, would have passed him. However, now they had to fall back some and try to come back around on the outside. When they did that, Winkfield was ready and pushed them out into the same deep sand where Abe Frank had already met with disastrous difficulty. Riding in this fashion, Winkfield was able to hold on in spite of his horse's injury and win the race by just a nose over the second-place horse, Inventor.

Winkfield had now won two Kentucky Derbies in a row, a record he could share with Isaac Murphy. But he was eager to set a new record, win three Kentucky Derbies in a row and also tie Murphy's record of three, for most total Derby victories by one jockey. Winkfield had a very good chance of doing just that in the 1903 Derby where he would be riding Early, the horse that was favored to win. As was his custom, Winkfield took Early out fast, setting the pace until the final quarter of the race. But he underestimated Judge Himes, a horse that had had only one victory in 10 races as a two-year-old. As Early was tiring, Judge Himes was able to slip inside on the rail while Winkfield was concentrating on two other horses. By the time Winkfield saw exactly what Judge Himes was doing, it was too late for him to summon Early to fend off the charge, and he wound up losing the race by three-quarters of a length.

When the 1904 Derby rolled around, Winkfield was just 21 years old and probably not yet even in his prime as a rider. But he would not be entered in this Derby, for reasons that are at best unclear. In later years, Wink declared that trying to meet his racing weight had become too much of a problem. But in saying that, the jockey may have simply been trying to avoid further repercussions from an incident that occurred only months after the Derby of 1903. Having become, by then, a highly sought after rider, he sometimes had the task of deciding which owner's offer to accept for a particular race. Historian Peter Chew gives this depiction of what happened on one occasion:

> Winkfield had a sharp eye for the main chance, and he went where the most money was, without thinking of the future. In the fall of 1903, he had promised to ride a horse for John E. Madden. When a bigger payment was offered him to ride the favorite in the race, he told Madden he'd forgotten and promised to ride for someone else. Winkfield finished up the track, the Madden horse came in third. After the race, Madden told Winkfield he didn't like to be double-crossed and that his name was going to be mud around the racetrack.[4]

It is hard to say whether or not Winkfield actually promised Madden that he would ride for him, and then reneged on that promise. But knowing how the jockey had conducted his entire career, determined to win at all costs, trying to be as profitable as possible in the process, it is not so difficult to speculate that he might have betrayed Madden in just the manner that Chew described, and then fled the country, having been blacklisted and maybe even having been threatened with bodily harm.

His immediate destination was Russia, where he rode for oil magnates, noblemen, and was thought to have even ridden for Czar Nicholas in those pre-Revolutionary times. While the thought of Winkfield racing for a Russian czar is an intriguing one, Chew contends that such could not have been the case because "Czar Nicholas had a small stable, horses of poor quality in Winkfield's view, and a reputation for paying poorly, so [he] never rode for the Czar, though legend has it that he did."[5] At any rate, he rode for six years in Russia, racking up one victory after another, and then for another three years for some of the wealthiest men in Austria-Hungary, including Prince Lubormoriski. Afterwards, he returned to Russia where he took up once again riding for some of the richest men in that country.

With the advent of the Russian Revolution, Winkfield and the aristocracy that he served became targets of the Bolsheviks and he found himself literally crawling on his hands and knees for hours in a daring escape. That escape was successful and he made his way to Poland and then France where he continued his career, riding not only in France but also in England, Spain, and other countries, garnering a reputation as the greatest jockey in all of Europe over a period of 20 years. In 1930, he finally retired from riding and took up working as a trainer, eventually acquiring his own stables in Maisons-Laffitte, just outside of Paris.

By the time Winkfield arrived in Maisons-Laffitte, Ernest Hemingway had already immortalized the town to some extent in a short story entitled "My Old Man." The youthful narrator in that literary work describes that "Maisons is about the swellest place to live I've ever seen in all my life. The town ain't so much, but there's a lake and a swell forest that we used to go off bumming in all day."[6] Indeed the town itself is small but nevertheless at the heart of a region well-known for breeding and training horses for events held throughout France. Hemingway's narrator reflects on how by the 1920s, Maisons-Laffitte had become a place where quite a few jockeys had migrated in their declining years. Concerning the father of the narrator's Maisons-Laffitte experience:

> There were lots of guys he'd known when he rode up at Paris, before the war, lived at Maisons, and there's a lot of time to sit around because the work around a racing stable, for the jocks, that is, is all cleaned up by nine o'clock in the morning. They take the first bunch of skins out to gallop at 5:30 in the morning and they work the second lot at 8 o'clock. That means getting up early all right and going to bed early, too.... [I]f a jock ain't working he sits around the Cafe de Paris with the gang and they can all sit around about two or three hours in front of some drink like a vermouth and seltz and they talk and tell stories and shoot pool and it's sort of like a club or the Galleria in Milan.[7]

Such were the goings-on at the place where Winkfield chose to spend his post-jockey years.

It was an idyllic lifestyle there in the French countryside until Germany invaded, taking over his enterprise and forcing him to take flight yet again. He made his way back to the United States, where he trained horses, mostly for various Southern owners. During this time, he gave apprentice jockey William Hartack a horse to ride in a meet in West Virginia. Hartack of course would continue his development and himself go on to win five Kentucky Derbies.

After World War II, Winkfield returned to Maisons-Laffitte and rebuilt his home and the stables that he had been forced by the Nazis to abandon. There he lived out the remainder of his life surrounded by family and engaged in the sport that he loved. His son Robert had gone into business with him, training horses as his father had done for so many years. When James Winkfield died on March 23, 1974, he was 91 years old, extraordinary for a jockey who had endured the rigors of high stakes racing over a period of several decades. Indeed, the fact that he had raced until he was practically 50 years old is a testament to his excellent conditioning. Fortunately, he avoided the fate of so many other jockeys who succumbed to a brutal dieting routine that ended in their early deaths.

By the time Winkfield had reached the end of his riding career, he had won an astounding 2,600 races, mostly on two-year-old horses all across the European continent. Had he stayed in America, he almost certainly would have been in more Kentucky Derbies than the four that he actually ran in. As it turns out, he left the United States in 1903, but continued racing horses until 1930. One can only guess what his Derby record would have been had he remained in America for just half of the years that he continued riding in Europe. He might easily have been the greatest Derby jockey of his or any other era.

At the time that Winkfield left America, the Derby itself was changing significantly. Once again, a new management team was brought in, highly successful Louisville businessmen who sought to make the Downs more profitable after years of consistent financial losses. A new clubhouse was built, more social events were added, and indeed this new management ushered the Downs and the Derby into the era in which they both would be appreciated as being among the great American sporting institutions. Ironically, this new era was also the period that witnessed a significant decline in African American jockey participation. From 1875 to 1902, blacks had won most of the Derbies. After that, no black jockey would win again for at least 100 years.

Perhaps the most profound testament to the tragedy of Winkfield with regard to American horseracing concerns an incident that occurred when the jockey returned to America to undergo a medical procedure in 1960 and wound up staying for the duration of the winter at his daughter Lillian's residence in Cincinnati, Ohio. While here in the States, he figured that he might as well go to nearby Louisville and take in the 1961 running of the Kentucky Derby. Having learned that the elderly Winkfield might be making the trip from Cincinnati to Louisville, members of the Turf Writers Association eagerly awaited in hopes of honoring him with a banquet at the prestigious Brown Hotel.

Winkfield did indeed make the trip and was on hand to witness the very Derby that he himself had won 59 years earlier. And he did show up at the Brown Hotel for the banquet at which he was to be the guest of honor. The problem was that when he came to the front door of that hotel, he was summarily told that he could not use the front door because he was black. The customs of the Old South had not disappeared in spite of the fact that seven years earlier, in 1954, the United States Supreme Court had ruled in *Brown v. Board of Education* that integration was to be the law of the land insofar as public accommodations were concerned. Winkfield, embarrassed, wound up waiting outside while Derby officials and members of the Turf Writers Association pleaded his case until the hotel finally made an exception and he was allowed to come in through the front entrance.

It was essential that he enter the hotel through the front door. One can only imagine how it would have been if he had had to come through the back door in order to participate in a ceremony arranged to honor him as a great American jockey. If such had occurred it would have amounted to as profound a paradox as what had occurred to Hattie McDaniel in 1940 when she was invited to the Academy Awards to pick up her Oscar for best supporting actress. As it turns out she was allowed to participate on the condition that she and her black guest sit at a table isolated in a corner away from the other honored guests, all of whom were white. She handled the situation gracefully and remained at the ceremony to receive her award. Yet, the message delivered to her in no uncertain terms was that however gifted she might have been as an actress, she would never be fully accepted even at the very ceremony that had been originally conceived to honor just the sort of talent which she possessed.

At one time in America, blacks riding horses in major stakes races were a common sight, during slavery and then for three decades after the Civil War had ended. As the sport gained increasing prominence, so did the jobs of trainers and jockeys become prestigious occupations. It was a paradoxical phenomenon—blacks who by the very definition of postbellum society accorded the status of second-class citizens even while they achieved a heralded status within the realm of America's national sport. Experiences such as what happened at the Brown Hotel must certainly have occurred quite frequently until there were virtually no black jockeys left to expose the social contradiction. As for Winkfield, after the Brown Hotel incident, he returned to France in the full belief that this was where he should go in order to be able to take the best advantage of his racing-related skills.

Conclusion

During the golden era of black jockeys in America, Kentucky produced more than its share of these gifted riders. From Oliver Lewis' Derby win in 1875, to James Winkfield's victory in 1902, Americans witnessed an extraordinary chain of black participation in what is now acknowledged as one of the world's premier equestrian events. Kentucky would produce other black jockeys during that era, other than the ones expounded upon in the preceding chapters, who nevertheless performed great feats in the field of racing though they never got to race in the Kentucky Derby. One such individual was Bud Haggins, who was born in 1870, and began exercising horses when he was just 11 years old. By the time he was 14, he was already winning races, 15 in a row aboard a horse named Little Fred who was owned by William Stoops. And there would be other winning rides for Haggins, some of which took place at Churchill Downs on horses such as Warrenton and Glenbrook.

As opportunities declined for African Americans in the flat racing events, Haggins joined other black jockeys venturing into the field of steeplechase racing. Arthur Ashe describes:

> After being forced out of "flat" racing, as events like the Kentucky Derby are called, some black riders turned to the steeplechase. Instead of racing around a flat track, horse and rider wind their way around a longer course beset with obstacles of various kinds—water jumps, hedge rows, railings, and the like....
>
> Though not with the same luster as their flat-turf cousins, the black

steeplechasers represented creditably. It remains another example of excellence where opportunity beckoned.[1]

Of course, steeplechase racing was not nearly as popular as the flat racing events, especially when one considers the magnitude that the Kentucky Derby had acquired by the early twentieth century. Still, it was a way for many of those jockeys to stay involved in some form of racing, and much of the skill and daring that had been required for flat racing was important for steeplechase riding as well.

Also from Kentucky was a jockey named William Porter, who began his career as a 14-year-old in 1891 with Edward Brown, the great African American horseman who was by then a highly reputable trainer and owner. After two years with Brown, Porter went on to ride for an illustrious array of other owners including Foxhall Keene, Albert Cox, William Landsberg, and E. J. "Lucky" Baldwin. Though he himself never rode in the Kentucky Derby, Porter did on various occasions get the opportunity to ride on some of the very horses who had competed in that event, including The Winner, which William Walker rode in the 1896 Derby.

Like Porter, John H. Jackson was born in Lexington, which by the 1890s had become an incredible mecca of black jockey talent. Jackson had been born two years after Porter, but by 1894, he was an exercise rider and then only six months after he had begun exercising horses, he began his career as a jockey. He continued his rapid development and had his best year in 1895, riding for Samuel C. Wagner. That was the year that he won an astounding 40 out of the 150 races in which he participated. He also had excellent years in 1896 and 1897, for the owners J. R. Bradley and J. A. Bennett, respectively. As the decade drew to a close, Jackson's career likewise began to wind down. His athletic gifts were fading as were the number of mounts that he was being offered for the important races.

Yet another extraordinary black jockey of the 1890s was Isaac Murphy's good friend Anthony Hamilton. The list of owners for whom the latter jockey rode could make up a who's who of horseracing dignitaries, including such men as William Lakeland, James Ben Ali Haggin, Senator George Hearst, Mike Dwyer, Pierre Lorillard, James R. Keene, and August Belmont Sr. and Jr. Though he never raced in the Kentucky Derby, he was certainly one of the more highly regarded jockeys of his era, winning such races as the St. Louis Derby in Missouri and the Metropolitan Handicap, the Gazelle Stakes, the Futurity Stakes, and the Lawrence Realization, those last four races all in the New York City area.

In addition to the excellent black jockeys who never raced in the Kentucky Derby, there would be other black jockeys who, after Winkfield, would race in the Derby but without a win. One such athlete was Jimmy Lee, who had a reputation for such fearlessness on the track that he, like Anthony Hamilton, was often referred to as "the black demon." Born in Graceland, Louisiana, Lee began exercising horses in 1901, just a few years before Winkfield left the United States to race overseas. In 1907, Lee got his chance to compete in the Kentucky Derby but could only manage a sixth-place finish. The next month, however, at Churchill Downs, he would sweep an entire six-race card and thereby re-establish himself as one of the country's top riders. The following two years he again got mounts for the Kentucky Derby, but on both occasions he turned out to be less than impressive. Yet his record in general was brilliant with wins in events such as the Kentucky Oaks at Churchill Downs, the Latonia Oaks, the Latonia Derby, and the Travers Stakes at Saratoga. The jockeys Alonzo Clayton, James Perkins, Willie Simms, and James Winkfield had won one or another of those same races throughout the years.

In 1907, Lee won the prestigious Clipsetta Stakes, in Latonia, Kentucky, an event that John Stoval, Ike Murphy, Samuel "Pike" Barnes, Tom Britton, Monk Overton, and "Tiny" Williams all had won before him. In fact, a jockey named Dale Austin had also won the Clipsetta Stakes before Lee did. Austin won the year before, in 1906. Also in 1906, Austin won the Latonia Oaks just one year ahead of Lee. In 1905, Austin won the Kentucky Oaks; the next black jockey to accomplish that feat would be Lee in 1907. These two contemporaries would be among the last few African American jockeys to compete in the most prestigious events in horseracing in America.

The 1907 Kentucky Derby actually saw Austin come in two horses ahead of Lee. Then in the 1909 Derby, Austin came in two horses ahead of Lee again. In all, Austin rode in this event six times between 1904 and 1910. The sheer number of times that he rode places him in the company of other black jockeys such as Stoval, who rode in the Derby six times and Overton, who rode eight times. All three of those jockeys, as great as they were, never won this particular race. Yet they made a crucial contribution to the Derby in terms of a competitive consistency the likes of which, other than in the case of Isaac Murphy, would not be seen again until the arrival of Earl Sande in the 1920s and 1930s aboard horses such as Zev, Flying Ebony, and Gallant Fox, and Eddie Arcaro himself in the 1930s, 1940s, and 1950s aboard horses such as Whirlaway, Hill Gail, and Citation.

Austin hung up his silks for good in 1911, but continued to exercise horses up to the day he died. He had begun his career with Thomas P. Hayes, and that would be the owner with whom his career and life would

Conclusion

Jimmy Lee (courtesy of the Keeneland Library).

end. One day in 1933, Austin had exercised horses at the Kentucky Association course in Lexington, and the next day he was found dead in his room at Hayes' barn on the grounds of that Lexington facility. His involvement with the Kentucky Derby was of profound significance, but equally phenomenal were his overall riding records for the years 1904 and 1906 when he won 137 and 142 races, respectively. In his prime he was known as the best jockey alive when it came to riding two-year-old horses. At his death, he was reputed to have won some race or another on every racetrack in the United States and Canada.

Just as Austin was retiring, black jockey Jess Conley was gearing up to make his way to the starting line for the 1911 Kentucky Derby. Conley had already participated in two previous Derbies, in 1898 and 1899, finishing last in that first run and third from among the five horses that were entered in 1899. In those last two Derbies of the nineteenth century, Conley had been competing against the likes of Willie Simms and Monk Overton, but such races with black jockeys primarily competing against one another were already coming to be a thing of the past.

By the time he made his Derby run in 1911, Conley was the only black rider among the seven jockeys entered. The horse that he would ride was Colston, named after the owner Raleigh Colston whose own Derby legacy was rather remarkable. He had ridden Searcher in the very first Derby of 1875, and then he rode Leamingtonian in the Derby the following year. In the first race he came in fifth out of the 15 who were entered, and the following year he finished in eighth place from among the 11 entrants. Colston would continue riding for several more years but it would be as a trainer that he would achieve his first Kentucky Derby win in 1883, with the Jack Chinn and G. W. Morgan-owned Leonatus.

Although Conley was Derby-tested, he not only was not on the horse that was favored to win, but according to the author Lynn Renau, "At the time of 'Soup' Perkins' death people still remembered that Colston's

Colston ran third in the 1911 Derby, badly ridden by Jess 'Long Shot' Conley, an African American everybody agreed was simply not up to the job."[2] It was a controversial race with some believing that the jockey who rode the favorite, Governor Gray, had actually "thrown" the race so that Meridian, who was considered the only other serious contender, could win. Colston was not considered in the same class with Meridian and Governor Gray, and his rider, Conley, having been away from the Derby for more than a decade, was thought to be no longer in his racing prime.

By the time of the 1921 Kentucky Derby there were very few blacks left among the ranks of American jockeys. The field of 12 horses this year included Planet who was ridden by the African American Henry King. King's 10th-place finish would be the last time a Derby crowd would see a black jockey riding in the event for another 79 years.

The reason why there was such a long lull in black jockey participation in this event is open to much speculation. In a 1995 article entitled "A Proud Derby Past, a Meager Present," the *St. Petersburg Times* noted:

> The diminution is partly the result of migration, blacks moving from the South and from small towns to the bigger cities in the North. They got away from their roots and no longer had the skills handed down from one generation to another. Tracks usually aren't in the big cities, so there were fewer blacks remaining to stay interested and to pass along the training.[3]

Robert Frister, writing for *Ebony* magazine in 1989, offers that same possibility, saying that "industrialization—migration from the farms to Northern cities—explains some of the thinning of the field of Black jockeys. Many great reinsmen, born and raised on the Kentucky farms where their fathers and forefathers had groomed and trained thoroughbreds, decided to seek a better life in the North."[4] There is much to be said for that perspective. In a sense, writer Ralph Ellison's classic novel, *Invisible Man*, is concerned with how black individuals can migrate to the North, lose their connection to their Southern roots, and thereby sacrifice their collective identity. Much of the dilemma for Ellison involved a desire to move beyond the vestiges of slavery without giving up the great strengths that blacks had acquired in the very midst of that peculiar institution. Many blacks indeed simply left the region of their birth and considered their newfound freedom to be more than enough of a trade-off for the oppressive conditions which they were leaving.

And yet when it comes to, as Frister calls them, the "great reinsmen" of Kentucky, one is inclined to ponder if it was really just a matter of wanting to go North that so thoroughly decimated what once was a large group of African American jockeys. For if indeed some were making upwards of $10,000 a year in the 1890s, a phenomenal salary in those days, then why would they not want to pass on the skills for that livelihood to their children and other young blacks for whom the North could certainly offer no greater prospects? Why would an established black jockey himself want to leave? Or to put it another way, what really happened to James Winkfield to make him choose racing in Russia over continuing an illustrious career on American soil? Northern migration was certainly one factor involved in the virtual disappearance of blacks from the jockey profession, but it does not tell the whole story.

It is fascinating to consider how shortly after that disappearance came the arrival of a new breed of jockey. In a 1961 *Sports Illustrated* article ironically entitled "Wanted: Good Jockeys," Whitney Tower assesses that:

> American boys are larger than they used to be. Modern riders start off with a size and weight disadvantage that ends many a career before it has properly begun. Then there are the child labor laws, which generally prohibit employment before the age of 16.
>
> Thus, unless a boy has been fortunate enough to gain experience on western stock or range horses, much of his enthusiasm is thwarted at just the period in his life when he is most readily susceptible to encouragement. In Latin America, because there are few school and labor regulations, boys get an early start in horsemanship and in actual raceriding competition.[5]

It all sounds so familiar. Black boys during and after slavery might start their riding careers at 11 or 12 years of age. Some were even younger. The paradox is that while there were no child labor laws to protect them, the very absence of such laws enabled them to become seasoned jockeys, winning events such as the Kentucky Derby at an age earlier than what modern laws would have even allowed them to ride at all.

Just as many blacks at one time had little opportunity for any real education or socioeconomic advancement in America, such was also the case in Mexico, Panama, and other Spanish-speaking countries where sometimes the only hope for a better life rested on the mere dreams of children strong enough and brave enough to climb up on the back of a horse and throw themselves into the fury of a high stakes racing event. The odds were long but then, as many a former black slave must himself have also concluded, what would have been the alternative? A life of poverty, most likely. And once in the saddle, that old traumatic life, thought to have been left behind, still loomed like a shadow threatening to hurl them back into that world from which they had only just recently escaped.

William Leggett, in another *Sports Illustrated* article, termed it the "Latin invasion," reiterating "that the American standard of living produces fewer and fewer small-sized boys. On the other hand, large numbers of Latin American youngsters are born and raised hungry, both in the literal sense and from the viewpoint of opportunities."[6] By the 1930s, instead of blacks, there was a new "hungry" outsider on the racing scene. And he would evolve into men with names like Arcaro, Cordero, and Valenzuela. These would be the new breed of underdog, literally hungry when they began, with nothing to lose but a history of stunted growth and wilted expectations. Meanwhile, as the theory goes, African Americans in general were no longer as small as they once were. The increasingly high American standard of living was in some sense the culprit limiting the pool of blacks who might otherwise be interested in horseracing.

Other perspectives on the contemporary shortage of black jockeys point to something more nefarious and systematic. Law professor Winkfield Twyman asserts that "the rules were changed so that entry into the business required educational credentials and sponsors. As a result, black jockeys were eased out of the profession over time."[7] Twyman compares the situation of black jockeys with that of black barbers who proliferated in America during the nineteenth century. Just as at one time the overwhelming majority of jockeys in the South were black, most barbers in the South were black too, both those who had a white clientele and those who serviced black customers. The barbering profession as a whole was deemed appropriate for blacks to be involved in since it was in essence just menial work. In Charlottesville, Virginia, for example, at one time

> There was only one barbershop that was run by a white man for whites. The rest of the barbershops, that were frequented by whites, were run for whites, but run by blacks ... those men made a decent living, a good living, running those barbershops. But then the white man found out that there was a piece of living in operating a barbershop, and they started passing those laws. You see, before then, you could come and work for me, and I would teach you how to be a barber. You may not be able to read and write, but you could be a good barber. But then they passed laws where you had to take an examination, and ... these white shops started opening up.[8]

In the nineteenth and early twentieth centuries, the sight of a black man trimming a white man's hair and shaving his face was a commonplace occurrence, even during the era of legal segregation. But as some of those black barbers began amassing great fortunes, forces came into play to put them out of business. Cutting the hair of influential white men had become too lucrative an endeavor to be dominated by blacks who were not supposed to be advancing but so high in the socioeconomic spectrum.

Attorney David Bernstein cites several professions in which this shift in racial dominance occurred, particularly during the 1890s and the early 1900s. In Ohio, during the late nineteenth century, black plumbers could be found in abundance. Plumbing had long been considered dirty work until it became obvious that it was nonetheless work for which one could be quite well paid. As had occurred in the situation of barbers, exclusively white licensing organizations began springing up in the plumbing profession and all but eliminated black participation. Cleveland, Ohio, which once had had numerous black plumbers, by 1910 had only five black plumbers who held one of these licenses.

The situation was even worse in other places, as Bernstein further informs.

> A 1953 state investigation disclosed that out of 3,200 licensed plumbers in Maryland, only two were black. The first black passed a plumbers' licensing exam in Colorado in 1950—and only after pressure from civil rights authorities. Only one black plumber was licensed in Charlotte, North Carolina in 1968. As late as 1972, only one black plumber was licensed in all of Montgomery County, Alabama, and he was only able to get his license after a ferocious struggle with the local plumbers' union. By the early 1970s, very few black plumbers were licensed in the United States.[9]

It might be surmised that as more opportunities opened up for blacks in other fields, they were no longer all that much interested in just being plumbers. That is similar to the view offered by those who believe that the current absence of black jockeys is due to increased opportunities away from Southern farms and instead in the Northern cities. Yet a question remains concerning how these fields, in which licensing developed, have attracted whites who were once not all that interested, while blacks who were once the mainstays of these professions have virtually disappeared. It is hard to believe that these fields, however lucrative, are just not the sort of work that African Americans any longer wish to do.

As far as horseracing was concerned, Arthur Ashe points to a seminal event that was, in 1894, the formation of the Jockey Club which had as one of its objectives to license and relicense jockeys. A resentment had grown on the part of many whites who had to watch the astounding success of many black jockeys who even then were continuing to build on a tradition of other black athletes who had performed so well previously in the sport. According to Ashe, the Jockey Club served the function of

systematically denying licenses to black riders who at this point in history must have known already that they were no longer welcome on the very racetracks that they had once dominated.

The author Charles Parmer argues that there is a distinction to be made between blacks who were racing in the East during the first decade of the twentieth century and blacks who were racing elsewhere. According to Parmer, the Eastern black jockeys became a "trifle cocky in the jockey rooms" and

> The white boys retaliated by ganging up against the black riders on the trails. A black boy would be pocketed, thrust back in a race; or his mount would be bumped out of contention; or a white boy would run alongside, slip a foot under a black boy's stirrup, and toss him out of the saddle. Again, while ostensibly whipping their own horses those white fellows would slash out and cut the nearest Negro rider.... They literally ran the black boys off the tracks.[10]

Parmer points to a phenomenon that was beginning to occur with more and more frequency, but it was by no means limited to Eastern racing tracks. Lynn Renau observes that by 1900 jockeys were actually involved in a "race war" in Chicago "instigated by white riders jealous of the success of so many African Americans ... [and resulting] in rough riding, fines and suspensions."[11] Renau further informs that there were "similar problems" in Latonia, Kentucky, the year before. In the past, blacks had been just as capable as anyone else of reckless riding. It will be remembered that in his very first race, James Winkfield cut across three other horses, causing a four-horse pileup that landed him a one-year suspension. In fact, one of the more effective racing strategies for a jockey, black or white, was to pocket or bump another jockey's horse in order to gain the advantage, particularly if that other horse was a decidedly better racehorse. For some jockeys, it was the only way they would ever get a chance to win. The fact that they would otherwise be almost certain to lose made it logical that they would take the chance and risk getting charged with a foul.

But the tactic seems to have taken on an increasingly racial motive. By the mid-1910s, a pattern was becoming so evident that fiction writer Charles E. Van Loan was compelled to comment on such occurrences in his popular horseracing stories. In "Playing Even for Obadiah" (1915), the white owner Old Man Curry has employed a black jockey but at the same time laments, "These judges won't give a nigger any the best of it on a claim of foul agin a white boy. My Mose is the only darky rider here, and the other boys want to drive him out."[12] In another Van Loan story, "A

106 Conclusion

Jockey fouled early in the twentieth century in an effort to deter him and other blacks from riding (drawing by F. C. Yohn for *Collier's*, 1915).

Morning Workout" (1916), black jockey Moseby Jones finds himself, in the midst of a race, first pocketed and then yelled at, "Niggeh … take 'at oat hound home 'e long way; you sutny neveh git him th'oo!"[13] Sure enough, Moseby never does get out of the pocket and because of that, he is only able to get a fourth-place finish.

Afterwards, Old Man Curry questions Jones about what the judges said when he told them he had been fouled. Jones, exasperated, declares:

> I done claim *three* fouls! Judges, they say they didn't see no foul a-a-a-tall! Didn't see us git bumped; didn't see Jock Merritt hit 'Lijah; didn't see us pocketed. 'Course they didn't; they wasn't *lookin'* faw no foul! On 'is track we not on'y got to beat hawsses; we got to beat jocks an' judges too.[14]

As it turns out, Merritt had intentionally smacked Jones' horse across the nose and then two other white jockeys moved over to further keep that black jockey's horse from advancing. None of this would the judges even acknowledge had occurred. It has been argued that it was not racism that ended the reign of black jockeys in high stakes races, for where large sums of money are concerned, what owner would even care what the race of his jockey was? But if owners who used black jockeys had to endure such tactics, without any recourse to the judges themselves, then how long could even a fair-minded owner continue to employ a black jockey?

As black jockeys began fading from high stakes racing in the early 1900s, a stigma was becoming attached to them that would remain to some extent a century later. Karl Schmitt, vice-president for corporate communications at Churchill Downs, was interviewed by the *St. Petersburg Times* where he asserted that there are still many black grooms and trainers. It is not too difficult to believe that quite a few blacks continue to be grooms. The labor involved in that position is still regarded for the most part as menial. And there are probably on the whole quite a few trainers at various tracks around the country. But as far as the Kentucky Derby itself is concerned, since the 1930s there have only been three black trainers: Raymond White whose American Eagle came in 16th in 1944, Edison Gaines whose King Clover came in 13th in 1951, and most recently Hank Allen whose Northern Wolf came in 6th in 1989.

Since the 1930s, there have even been a handful of black owners who have had their horses entered in the Derby. Raleigh Colston's Colston had finished third in 1911, and entertainer Stanley "Hammer" Burrell's Dance Floor equaled that achievement in 1992. Before Dance Floor, Henry Greene's Partez had also finished third in 1981. Other black owners who have had horses entered in the Derby include comedian Eddie Anderson (1943), James Cottrell (1988), and music mogul Berry Gordy (1994). The accomplishments of those owners are certainly laudable, but their number is still profoundly low.

The sheer cost of owning a Derby-quality horse prevents many blacks from entering into horseracing. Burrell, a part-owner of Oaktown Stables, had a horse named Lite Light that won the Kentucky Oaks in 1992, the same year that Dance Floor placed third in the Derby. Dance Floor cost Burrell and his family $135,000 and Lite Light was reported to have cost somewhere between $500,000 and $1.2 million. Clearly, such costs prohibit all but the most wealthy from even thinking about buying a horse capable of winning the Kentucky Derby race.

As far as the jockeys themselves, Schmitt in the *St. Petersburg Times* interview seemed to accept the idea that the old farm system that had once produced great black jockeys is simply no longer the same. Says the Churchill Downs executive, "In racing, you have to work at it until you get a break—and then maybe you get some bad rides (slow horses) or someone doesn't like you or you get a bad reputation and you *still* don't make it. The whole system's different."[15] The selectivity involved, though, would make one think that blacks particularly might still be bypassed not for any lack of ability, but merely because of their race.

In "A Morning Workout," Old Man Curry, quoting the biblical Solomon, tells Moseby Jones that eventually he will get justice on the track, to which the jockey answers, "You kin take Sol'mun's word faw it, boss, but li'l Moseby, he's f'um Mizzoury. He'll steal a flyin' start nex' time out an' try to stay so far in front that no Irish boy kin reach him 'ith a lariat!"[16] Not so much caring to wait on Providence, the black jockey in that story maintains that whenever he races, he will simply take a commanding lead and never relinquish it, thus making sure that no group of white riders can foul him into submission and defeat.

The question, though, becomes how likely is it that Jones' strategy will be successful against the vast wave of sentiment that would preclude him from not only winning but even being entered in important races. How long, if ever, can he manage to stay ahead of his nemeses? The very fact that he has been reduced to having a "flyin' start" as his only strategy has already sealed his competitive fate because as we have already seen in earlier chapters, a significant number of races cannot be won that way. In Jones' case, he soon will be forced to hang up his silks from the sheer weight of all the obstacles.

Some would argue that the obstacles still remain. Carl Williams, a contemporary black jockey who does most of his riding at Tampa Bay Downs in Florida, contends that

> Skin color still has an impact on who gets to ride and who doesn't.
> You know how it is as far as being black. Not everybody's prejudiced, but it's hard.... I've had a lot of trainers come up to me and tell me, "You can ride as good as anybody else and you try hard, but...." They never call me names but they let me know it's a matter of color.
> I don't get that many rides.[17]

Williams' is only one perspective. Perhaps the problem, as Schmitt suggests, is that blacks are no longer as integral to the horse farming system as they once were. Or perhaps blacks in general are physically much larger in size, and that can explain our absence from the world of high stakes racing competition. On the other hand, Williams' testimony points to what might be the biggest obstacle of all. Now that the black presence among heralded jockeys is so severely small, the stigma itself of that lengthy absence, especially from events like the Derby, makes the barriers to renewed participation extremely difficult to climb even though the climb back is a task that is necessary to undertake.

In 1995, just a week before that year's Kentucky Derby, a confident but yet disappointed young jockey named Marlon St. Julien was quoted in the *Atlanta Journal-Constitution* as saying, "I'm not bragging on myself.... I have a lot of compliments on my riding. But I have a lot of jockey friends who are white who have moved on to bigger tracks. A lot of trainers might not ride me because I am black, but that's a personal opinion."[18] At 23 years old, St. Julien even then was an excellent jockey who was nonetheless limited to certain Louisiana racetracks.

Five years later, he became the first African American to ride in the Kentucky Derby in 79 years. It had been 98 years since an African American had won. The day before his historic ride, St. Julien declared, "I just want to be considered as one of the best riders in the country, whether black, white, purple, blue or brown."[19] Among his competitors would be Pat Day, Chris McCarron, and Craig Perret, all of whom had won the Derby before. The eventual winner of the Derby of 2000, Fusaichi Pegasus, had been purchased as a yearling for an astounding $4 million. St. Julien had made it into the race of his life, and although he had said that he just wanted to be regarded as one of the best jockeys in America regardless of color, his horse Curule was carrying not only St. Julien but also the weight of a curious history. When that horse came across the finish line in seventh place out of 19 entries, St. Julien had proven his point, that he is among the best in the world and color should never have mattered.

Yet race does continue to matter even on into the twenty-first century. In 2001, the year immediately following St. Julien's momentous ride, *USA Today* described racial tensions in Louisville that threatened to detract from the celebratory atmosphere of the 127th running.[20] Earlier that year, Cincinnati had been embroiled in controversy over the police-related deaths of 15 young black men within a five-year period.

Louisville, just 90 minutes away from Cincinnati, had its own similar problems. In 1999, two police officers shot and killed an unarmed black teenager who it was later said had tried to run them over with a stolen car. The officers involved received medals of valor for their participation in that episode. But as *USA Today* further reported, the mayor of Louisville wound up firing his own police chief for having approved the awarding of those medals under such controversial circumstances. That act on the part of the mayor is evidence that Louisville still has much work to do in the area of race relations.

The celebrations surrounding Derby Day remain largely segregated. On one side of town the predominantly white $800-a-couple Lexington Ball and $300-a-ticket Mint Jubilee are held while the predominantly African American West End section of town engages itself in a regular yearly ritual whereupon 150,000 to 200,000 people cruise in cars and party along the streets, an occurrence that in the year 2000 led to the issuing of hundreds of citations and arrests. It is quite a commentary on the racial disparity that exists even in the city where the Kentucky Derby once held so much promise for African Americans.

In recent years, there has evolved a need to reassess the role that blacks play not just with regard to the Derby but with regard to the city of Louisville in general. January 2001 saw yet another black teenager fatally shot with the familiar explanation offered that he had tried to run over an officer. The regularity of such incidents has led to the creation of groups such as the Kentucky Alliance Against Racist and Political Repression as well as a commission appointed by Louisville's mayor for the expressed purpose of studying race relations. Dignitaries from around the world have traveled to Louisville to witness the Kentucky Derby. But now that event has, in addition, become a site where activists as varied as Martin Luther King III, Dick Gregory, and the Reverend Al Sharpton render their various warnings concerning the city's racial climate. The Derby has been turned into an effective platform whereby disenchanted blacks can regularly proclaim the extent to which racism has yet to be overcome.

APPENDIX A

Summary of Black Kentucky Derby Winners

Date	Jockey	Horse	Time
May 17, 1875	Oliver Lewis	Aristides	2:37¾
May 22, 1877	William Walker	Baden-Baden	2:38
May 21, 1878	James Carter	Day Star	2:37¼
May 18, 1880	George Lewis	Fonso	2:37½
May 16, 1882	"Babe" Hurd	Apollo	2:40¼
May 16, 1884	Isaac Murphy	Buchanan	2:40¼
May 14, 1885	E. Henderson	Joe Cotton	2:37¼
May 11, 1887	Isaac Lewis	Montrose	2:39¼
May 14, 1890	Isaac Murphy	Riley	2:45
May 13, 1891	Isaac Murphy	Kingman	2:52¼
May 11, 1892	Alonzo Clayton	Azra	2:41½
May 6, 1895	James Perkins	Halma	2:37½
May 6, 1896	Willie Simms	Ben Brush	2:07¾
May 4, 1898	Willie Simms	Plaudit	2:09
Apr. 29, 1901	James Winkfield	His Eminence	2:07¾
May 3, 1902	James Winkfield	Alan-a-Dale	2:08¾

APPENDIX B

BLACK OWNERS OF KENTUCKY DERBY HORSES

Year	Owner	Horse	Place
1880	Milton Young	Bancroft	3rd
1881	Milton Young	Getaway	5th
1882	Milton Young	Lost Cause	13th
1889	Milton Young	Once Again	3rd
1885	Milton Young	Ten Booker	3rd
1891	Dudley Allen	Kingman	1st
1895	Byron McClelland	Halma	1st
1896	Edward Brown	Ulysses	8th
1911	Raleigh Colston	Colston	3rd
1943	Eddie Anderson	Burnt Cork	10th
1981	Henry Greene	Partez	3rd
1988	James Cottrell	Jim's Orbit	10th
1992	Stanley Burrell	Dance Floor	3rd
1994	Berry Gordy	Powis Castle	8th

APPENDIX C

BLACK TRAINERS OF KENTUCKY DERBY HORSES

Year	Trainer	Horse	Place
1875	Ansel Williamson	Aristides	1st
1876	James Williams	Vagrant	1st
1877	Edward Brown	Baden-Baden	1st
1883	Raleigh Colston	Leonatus	1st
1884	William Bird	Buchanan	1st
1885	Alex Perry	Joe Cotton	1st
1891	Dudley Allen	Kingman	1st
1896	Edward Brown	Ulysses	8th
1913	C. Banks	Ten Point	2nd
1914	William Buckner	Old Ben	5th
1915	Will Perkins	Tetan	14th
1921	Will Perkins	Uncle Velo	8th
1922	Will Perkins	John Finn	3rd
1925	Will Perkins	Son of John	3rd
1925	Will Perkins	Step Along	5th
1928	William Buckner	Bar None	12th
1932	Raymond White	Crystal Prince	12th

Appendix C: Black Trainers of Kentucky Derby Horses

Year	Trainer	Horse	Place
1932	William Buckner	Oscillation	13th
1934	Marshall Lilly	Spy Hill	6th
1944	Raymond White	American Eagle	16th
1951	Edison Gaines	King Clover	13th
1989	Hank Allen	Northern Wolf	6th

NOTES

Introduction

1. Flannery O'Connor, "The Artificial Nigger," in *A Good Man Is Hard to Find and Other Stories* (1955; New York: Harcourt, reprinted 1977), 128.
2. Williston Hough, "The Palio of Siena: A Curious Medieval Horse-Race," *Outlook*, 22 July 1905, p. 756.
3. Hough 756.
4. Jesse Lynch Williams, "Saratoga and Its People," *Outing* 41 (1902), 266.
5. Hugh Logan, "Derby Day in England," *Munsey's Magazine* 27 (1902), 455.
6. Robin Law, *The Horse in West African History* (London: Oxford University Press, 1980), 76.
7. Charles B. Parmer, *For Gold and Glory* (New York: Carrick and Evans, 1939), 62.
8. Parmer 62.
9. Hotaling, Edward, *The Great Black Jockeys: The Lives and Times of the Men Who Dominated America's First National Sport* (Rocklin, California: Forum, 1999), 62.

I. *Oliver Lewis*

1. Charles E. Van Loan, "Leveling with Elisha," *Collier's*, 22 May 1915, p. 36, col. 3.
2. Matt J. Winn and Frank G. Menke, *Down the Stretch: The Story of Matt J. Winn* (New York: Smith and Durrell, 1945), 4–5.
3. George B. Leach, *The Kentucky Derby Diamond Jubilee* (Louisville: Gibbs-Inman, 1949), 17.

4. Betty Earle Borries, *Isaac Murphy: Kentucky's Record Jockey* (Berea, Kentucky: Kentucke Imprints, 1988), 1–2.
5. Peter Chew, *The Kentucky Derby: The First 100 Years* (Boston: Houghton Mifflin, 1974), 22.
6. Chew 23.
7. Edward Hotaling, "When Racing Colors Included Black," *New York Times*, 2 June 1996, sec. 8, p. 9, col. 3.
8. Charles Belmont Davis, "The American at Play," *Outing* 43 (1903), 267.
9. Leach 17.
10. "Derby Day," *Courier-Journal*, 18 May 1875, p. 4, col. 3.
11. Lynn S. Renau, *Racing Around Kentucky* (Louisville: Lynn S. Renau Antiques Consultant, 1995), 127–28.
12. Davis 268.
13. Davis 268.
14. Law 1.
15. Renau 128.
16. Renau 127.
17. Chew 23.
18. "Derby Day," p. 4, col. 2.
19. "Derby Day," p. 4, col. 2.
20. Hotaling, *The Great Black Jockeys: The Lives and Times of the Men Who Dominated America's First National Sport*, 231.
21. Winn 1.

II. William Walker

1. George C. Wright, *Racial Violence in Kentucky, 1865–1940: Lynchings, Mob Rule, and "Legal Lynchings"* (Baton Rouge: Louisiana State University Press, 1990), 132–33.
2. Wright 133.
3. Borries 7.
4. "A Day of Surprises," *Courier-Journal*, 23 May 1877, p. 4, col. 2.
5. Winn 7.
6. Winn 8.

III. James Carter

1. Leach 63.
2. Robert Wickliffe Woolley, "Old Kentucky and the Thoroughbred," *Outing* 36 (1900), 645.
3. "Darby!" *Courier-Journal*, 22 May 1878, p. 4, col. 2.
4. Beverley Bryant and Jean Williams, *Portraits in Roses: 109 Years of Kentucky Derby Winners* (New York: McGraw-Hill, 1984), 6.
5. Chew 13.
6. Leach 23.

IV. George Garrett Lewis

1. Renau 112–13.
2. "Fonso in Front," *Courier-Journal*, 19 May 1880, p. 4, col. 2.
3. Renau 113.
4. William Wells Brown, *My Southern Home* (1880; New York: Negro Universities Press, 1969), 177.
5. Brown 178.
6. "Fonso in Front," p. 4, col. 2.
7. Parmer 146.
8. "Fonso in Front," p. 4, col. 2.
9. Bryant and Williams 8.
10. "Fonso in Front," p. 4, col. 3.

V. "Babe" Hurd

1. Leach 30.
2. Booker T. Washington, *Up From Slavery* (1901; New York: Bantam, 1970), 156.
3. Chew 26.
4. Bruce Lowitt, "A Proud Derby Past, a Meager Present," *St. Petersburg Times*, 3 May 1995, sec. C, p. 5, col. 3.
5. Lowitt, sec. C, p. 5, col. 3.
6. Borries 14.
7. Winn 28–29.
8. "Apollo Wins," *Courier-Journal*, 17 May 1882, p. 6, col. 2.
9. "Apollo Wins," p. 6, col. 2.

VI. Erskine "Babe" Henderson

1. Woolley 645.
2. E. Merton Coulter, *The Civil War and Readjustment in Kentucky* (Gloucester, Massachusetts: Peter Smith, 1966), 224.
3. "Crowding the Record," *Courier-Journal*, 15 May 1885, p. 6, col. 2.
4. "Crowding the Record," p. 6, col. 2.
5. Wright 248.
6. Wright 249.
7. "The Great Event," *Courier-Journal*, 13 May 1885, p. 2, col. 6.
8. Renau 144.
9. Arna Bontemps, *God Sends Sunday* (1931; New York: Harcourt, 1972), 17–19.
10. Bontemps 103.
11. Bontemps 104.

VII. Isaac Lewis

1. Woolley 642.
2. Houston A. Baker, Jr. "This Is Not a Poem," in *Trouble the Water: 250 Years of African-American Poetry*, edited by Jerry W. Ward, Jr. (New York: Penguin, 1997), 491.
3. "Montrose First," *Courier-Journal*, 12 May 1887, p. 5, col. 2.
4. "Montrose First," p. 5, col. 2.

VIII. Isaac Murphy

1. Marvin Scott, *The Racing Game* (Chicago: Aldine, 1968), 27.
2. Borries 22.
3. Chew 38.
4. Hotaling, *The Great Black Jockeys: The Lives and Times of the Men Who Dominated America's First National Sport*, 280–81.
5. Renau 136.
6. Chew 37.
7. Borries 55.
8. Chew 30.
9. Borries 71.
10. "Riley's Race," *Courier-Journal*, 15 May 1890, p. 2, col. 2.
11. Borries 72.
12. Parmer 148.
13. "Riley's Race," p. 2, col. 1.
14. Chew 40.

IX. Alonzo Clayton

1. "Louisville Jockey Club Races," *Courier-Journal*, 12 May 1892, p. 6, col. 2.
2. Parmer 149.
3. "Louisville Jockey Club Races," p. 6, col. 3.
4. "Louisville Jockey Club Races," p. 6, col. 1.

X. James Perkins

1. Renau 138.
2. Winn 34–35.
3. "Crowned: Halma King of the Kentucky Turf," *Courier-Journal*, 7 May 1895, p. 2, col. 1.
4. "Crowned: Halma King of the Kentucky Turf," p. 2, col. 1.

XI. Willie Simms

1. Jonathan M. Bryant, "'We Have No Chance of Justice before the Courts': The Freedmen's Struggle for Power in Greene County, Georgia, 1865– 1874," in *Georgia in Black and White: Explorations in the Race Relations of a Southern State, 1865–1950*, edited by John C. Inscoe (Athens: University of Georgia Press, 1994), 25.
2. Russell Duncan, *Entrepreneur for Equality: Governor Rufus Bullock, Commerce, and Race in Post–Civil War Georgia* (Athens: University of Georgia Press, 1994), 75.
3. "By a Nose: Ben Brush Wins the Kentucky Derby," *Courier-Journal* 7 May 1896, p. 7, col. 1.
4. Elisha Warfield Kelly, "Our Horses and Jockeys Abroad," *Munsey's Magazine* 24 (1900), 362.
5. Kelly 362.
6. Kelly 357.
7. Kelly 353.
8. Kelly 358.
9. Kelly 354.
10. Arthur R. Ashe, Jr., *A Hard Road to Glory: A History of the African-American Athlete 1619–1918*, vol. 1 (1988; New York: Amistad, 1993), 49.
11. Ashe 44.
12. Ashe 44.
13. Hotaling, *The Great Black Jockeys: The Lives and Times of the Men Who Dominated America's First National Sport*, 297.
14. Hotaling, *The Great Black Jockeys: The Lives and Times of the Men Who Dominated America's First National Sport*, 298.
15. "Plessy v. Ferguson, 163 U.S. 537 (1896)" in *Race and Ethnic Relations 95/96*, edited by John A. Kromkowski (Guilford, Connecticut: Dushkin, 1995), 20.
16. "By a Nose: Ben Brush Wins the Kentucky Derby," p. 1, col. 4.
17. "By a Nose: Ben Brush Wins the Kentucky Derby," p. 7, col. 1.
18. "By a Nose: Ben Brush Wins the Kentucky Derby," p. 1, col. 6; p. 6, col. 1.
19. "The Royal Sport Begins: Twenty-Fourth Renewal of the Kentucky Derby This Afternoon," *Courier-Journal*, 4 May 1898, p. 6, col. 6.
20. "The Royal Sport Begins: Twenty-Fourth Renewal of the Kentucky Derby This Afternoon," p. 6, col. 6.
21. "Kentucky Conquers," *Courier-Journal*, 5 May 1898, p. 6, col. 8.

XII. James Winkfield

1. "His Eminence Wins the Twenty-Seventh Kentucky Derby," *Courier-Journal*, 30 April 1901, p. 2, col. 6.
2. "His Eminence Wins the Twenty-Seventh Kentucky Derby," p. 3, col. 3–4.
3. Chew 36.
4. Chew 36.

5. Chew 36–37.
6. Ernest Hemingway, "My Old Man," in *The Snows of Kilimanjaro and Other Stories* (1923; Harmondsworth, Middlesex: Penguin, reprinted 1963), 124.
7. Hemingway 125.

Conclusion

1. Ashe 51–52.
2. Renau 139.
3. Lowitt, sec. C, p. 5, col. 2.
4. Robert A. Frister, "Black Winners of the Kentucky Derby," *Ebony* 44 (1989), 87.
5. Whitney Tower, "Wanted: Good Jockeys," *Sports Illustrated*, 24 April 1961, p. 58.
6. William Leggett, "The Latin Invasion," *Sports Illustrated*, 5 February 1962, p. 14.
7. Winkfield F. Twyman, Jr., "A Critique of the California Civil Rights Initiative," *National Black Law Journal* 14 (1997), 186.
8. James Robert Saunders and Renae Nadine Shackelford, *Urban Renewal and the End of Black Culture in Charlottesville, Virginia: An Oral History of Vinegar Hill* (Jefferson, North Carolina: McFarland, 1998), 90.
9. David E. Bernstein, "Licensing Laws: A Historical Example of the Use of Government Regulatory Power Against African-Americans," *San Diego Law Review* 31 (1994), 98–99.
10. Parmer 150.
11. Renau 143.
12. Charles E. Van Loan, "Playing Even for Obadiah," *Collier's*, 26 June 1915, p. 5, col. 2.
13. Charles E. Van Loan, "A Morning Workout," *Collier's*, 15 April 1916, p. 5, col. 1.
14. Van Loan, "A Morning Workout," p. 5, col. 1.
15. Lowitt, sec. C, p. 5, col. 2.
16. Van Loan, "A Morning Workout," p. 5, col. 2.
17. Lowitt, sec. C, p. 5, col. 3.
18. Martha Woodham, "The Forgotten Riders," *Atlanta Journal-Constitution*, 30 April 1995, sec. N, p. 1, col. 3.
19. Ed Schuyler, Jr., "Derby Has as Many Story Lines as Horses," *Journal and Courier*, 6 May 2000, sec. C, p. 1, col. 2.
20. Kevin Davis, "Derby Party Unfolds Amid Racial Tensions: Protests Over Alleged Police Abuses Against Blacks to Accompany Toasts and Cheers in Kentucky," *USA Today*, 4 May 2001, sec. A, p. 3, col. 2.

BIBLIOGRAPHY

Ashe, Arthur R., Jr. *A Hard Road to Glory: A History of the African-American Athlete 1619–1918*. Vol. 1. 1988. New York: Amistad, 1993.
"Apollo Wins." *Courier-Journal*, 17 May 1882, 6.
Baker, Houston A., Jr. "This Is Not a Poem." In *Trouble the Water: 250 Years of African-American Poetry*, edited by Jerry W. Ward, Jr. (New York: Penguin, 1997), 491.
Bernstein, David E. "Licensing Laws: A Historical Example of the Use of Government Regulatory Power Against African-Americans." *San Diego Law Review* 31 (1994): 89–104.
Bontemps, Arna. *God Sends Sunday*. 1931. New York: Harcourt, 1972.
Borries, Betty Earle. *Isaac Murphy: Kentucky's Record Jockey*. Berea, Kentucky: Kentucke Imprints, 1988.
Brown, William Wells. *My Southern Home*. 1880. New York: Negro Universities Press, 1969.
Bryant, Beverley, and Jean Williams. *Portraits in Roses: 109 Years of Kentucky Derby Winners*. New York: McGraw-Hill, 1984.
Bryant, Jonathan M. "'We Have No Chance of Justice before the Courts': The Freedmen's Struggle for Power in Greene County, Georgia, 1865–1874." In *Georgia in Black and White: Explorations in the Race Relations of a Southern State*, edited by John C. Inscoe (Athens: University of Georgia Press, 1994), 13–37.
"By a Nose: Ben Brush Wins the Kentucky Derby." *Courier-Journal*, 7 May 1896, 7.
Chew, Peter. *The Kentucky Derby: The First 100 Years*. Boston: Houghton Mifflin, 1974.
Coulter, E. Merton. *The Civil War and Readjustment in Kentucky*. Gloucester, Massachusetts: Peter Smith, 1966.
"Crowding the Record." *Courier-Journal*, 15 May 1885, 6.
"Crowned: Halma King of the Kentucky Turf." *Courier-Journal*, 7 May 1895, 2.
"Darby!" *Courier-Journal*, 22 May 1878, 4.

Davis, Charles Belmont. "The American at Play." *Outing* 43 (1903): 261–71.
Davis, Kevin. "Derby Party Unfolds Amid Racial Tensions: Protests Over Alleged Police Abuses Against Blacks to Accompany Toasts and Cheers in Kentucky." *USA Today*, 4 May 2001, sec. A: 3.
"A Day of Surprises." *Courier-Journal*, 23 May 1877, 4.
"Derby Day." *Courier-Journal*, 18 May 1875, 4.
Duncan, Russell. *Entrepreneur for Equality: Governor Rufus Bullock, Commerce, and Race in Post–Civil War Georgia*. Athens: University of Georgia Press, 1994.
"Fonso in Front." *Courier-Journal* 19 May 1880, 4.
Frister, Robert A. "Black Winners of the Kentucky Derby." *Ebony* 44 (1989): 82–87.
"The Great Event." *Courier-Journal*, 13 May 1885, 2.
Hemingway, Ernest. "My Old Man." 1923. In *The Snows of Kilimanjaro and Other Stories* (Harmondsworth, Middlesex: Penguin, 1963), 119–35.
"His Eminence Wins the Twenty-Seventh Kentucky Derby." *Courier-Journal*, 30 April 1901, 2.
Hotaling, Edward. *The Great Black Jockeys: The Lives and Times of the Men Who Dominated America's First National Sport*. Rocklin, California: Forum, 1999.
———. "When Racing Colors Included Black." *New York Times*, 2 June 1996, sec. 8: 9.
Hough, Williston. "The Palio of Siena: A Curious Medieval Horse-Race." *Outlook*, 22 July 1905, 756–65.
Kelly, Elisha Warfield. "Our Horses and Jockeys Abroad." *Munsey's Magazine* 24 (1900): 253–63.
"Kentucky Conquers." *Courier-Journal*, 5 May 1898, 6.
Law, Robin. *The Horse in West African History*. London: Oxford University Press, 1980.
Leach, George B. *The Kentucky Derby Diamond Jubilee*. Louisville: Gibbs-Inman, 1949.
Leggett, William. "The Latin Invasion." *Sports Illustrated*, 5 February 1962, 12–15.
Logan, Hugh. "Derby Day in England." *Munsey's Magazine* 27 (1902): 450–56.
"Louisville Jockey Club Races." *Courier-Journal*, 12 May 1892, 6.
Lowitt, Bruce. "A Proud Derby Past, a Meager Present." *St. Petersburg Times*, 3 May 1995, sec. C: 5.
"Montrose First." *Courier-Journal*, 12 May 1887, 5.
O'Connor, Flannery. "The Artificial Nigger." 1955. In *A Good Man Is Hard to Find and Other Stories* (New York: Harcourt, 1977), 102–29.
Parmer, Charles B. *For Gold and Glory*. New York: Carrick and Evans, 1939.
"Plessy v. Ferguson, 163 U.S. 537 (1986)." In *Race and Ethnic Relations 95/96* (Guilford, Connecticut: Dushkin, 1995), 17–23.
Renau, Lynn S. *Racing Around Kentucky*. Louisville: Lynn S. Renau Antiques Consultant, 1995.
"Riley's Race." *Courier-Journal*, 15 May 1890, 2.
"The Royal Sport Begins: Twenty-Fourth Renewal of the Kentucky Derby This Afternoon." *Courier-Journal*, 4 May 1898, 6.
Saunders, James Robert, and Renae Nadine Shackelford. *Urban Renewal and the End of Black Culture in Charlottesville, Virginia: An Oral History of Vinegar Hill*. Jefferson, North Carolina: McFarland, 1998.
Schuyler, Ed, Jr. "Derby Has as Many Story Lines as Horses." *Journal and Courier*, 6 May 2000, sec. C: 1.

Scott, Marvin. *The Racing Game*. Chicago: Aldine, 1968.
Tower, Whitney. "Wanted: Good Jockeys." *Sports Illustrated*, 24 April 1961, 56–62.
Twyman, Winkfield F., Jr. "A Critique of the California Civil Rights Initiative." *National Black Law Journal* 14 (1997): 181–203.
Van Loan, Charles E. "Leveling with Elisha." *Collier's*, 22 May 1915, 36.
_____. "A Morning Workout." *Collier's*, 15 April 1916, 5.
_____. "Playing Even for Obadiah." *Collier's*, 26 June 1915, 5.
Washington, Booker T. *Up From Slavery*. 1901. New York: Bantam, 1970.
Williams, Jesse Lynch. "Saratoga and Its People." *Outing* 41 (1902): 265–75.
Winn, Matt J., and Frank G. Menke. *Down the Stretch: The Story of Matt J. Winn*. New York: Smith and Durrell, 1945.
Woodham, Martha. "The Forgotten Riders." *Atlanta Journal-Constitution*, 30 April 1995, sec. N: 1.
Woolley, Robert Wickliffe. "Old Kentucky and the Thoroughbred." *Outing* 36 (1900): 642–50.
Wright, George C. *Racial Violence in Kentucky, 1865–1940: Lynchings, Mob Rule, and "Legal Lynchings."* Baton Rouge: Louisiana State University Press, 1990.

INDEX

Abe, Frank 90–92
Admiral 56–57
Africa 4
Agile 66
Alabama Stakes 48
Alan-a-Dale 26, 90–92
Alard Scheck 88–89
Alexander, A. J. 38–39
Alexander, Robert A. 16, 38–39, 42, 84
Alexander Stakes 47
Ali, Muhammad 53
Allen, Dudley 63
Allen, Hank 107
American Derby 51
American Eagle 107
Amur 89
Anderson, Eddie 107
Apollo 35–37, 55
Arcaro, Eddie 51, 64–65, 99, 103
Archer, Fred 55–56, 59
Aristides 10–18, 39
"The Artificial Nigger" 1
Ascension 12, 30
Ashe, Arthur 12–13, 81, 97–98, 104–5
Ashland Stud Farm 26–27
Audrain 56
Austin, Dale 48, 66, 99–100
Azra 66–69

Babcock 34–36
Badejo, Diedre L. vii
Baden-Baden 21, 54, 84
Baldwin, Elias Jackson "Lucky" 59, 66, 98
Baker, Houston A., Jr. 45
Balgowan 63–64
Ban Yan 48
Banburg 45–46, 48
Bancroft 30–32, 54
Barnes, Samuel "Pike" 99
Barnes, W. S. 45
Bashford 63, 67, 69
Basso 75
Beck, James 20
Belmont, August, Jr. 98
Belmont, August, Sr. 98
Belmont Stakes 18, 78, 84, 86
Ben Ali 58
Ben Brush 82–84
Ben Eder 83, 85
Bennett, George C. 90
Bennett, J. A. 98
Berson 39–41, 57
Bernstein, David 104
Bible 107
Bill Letcher 60
Bird, William 57
Blaylock, H. 45

Index

Blue Ribbon Stakes 26, 45
Blue Wing 58
Bob Miles 56–57
Bob Wooley 19
Boland, Jimmy 87–89
Bolsheviks 93
Bombay 19
Bonnie Australian 57
Bontemps, Arna 42–43
Borries, Betty 11, 21, 34, 56
Boulevard 31
Bradley, J. R. 98
Bravo 28
Brighton Handicap 84
Britton, Thomas 23, 55, 67–70, 99
Brookful 49
Brown, Edward 21–22, 55, 82–84, 98
Brown, S. S. 66
Brown, William Wells 29–30
Brown Dick 83
Brown Hotel 95–96
Brown v. Board of Education 95
Buchanan 56–57, 61
Buford, Abe 47
Burns, James 51
Burns, Tom 85
Burrell, Stanley "Hammer" 107
Byrnes, Matt 61

Caesar 81
Cahn, J. C. 87
Calazzi Stables 44
California Handicap 71
Calvin 18
Campbell, Hardy 84
Carter, James 25–27
Cato 6
Cesarewitch 80–81
Chambers, H. 17
Champagne Stakes 66
Champion Stakes 58
Charade 78
Chatter 39
Chesapeake 10–11, 14–16, 40
Chew, Peter 12–13, 16–17, 27, 34, 56, 93
Chinese Exclusion Act 33
Chinn, Jack 100
Churchill, John 3
Churchill Henry 3
Cincinnati Hotel Handicap 45

Citation 51, 99
Civil War 39, 45, 51, 77, 82, 96
Clark, M. Lewis viii, 3, 34–35, 42, 74, 85
Clark Handicap 36, 48, 57, 71
Clark Stakes 69
Classmate 54
Clay, Henry 6, 26, 90
Clay, John M. 26–27
Clay, Woodford 88
Clayton, Alonzo 66–71, 74–76, 99
Clipsetta Stakes 48, 70, 99
Clyde Van Dusen 88
Coburn, Willie 90–92
Colston 100–1, 107
Colston, Raleigh 100, 107
Comanche 78
Coney Island Derby 39
Conley, Jess 48, 100–1
Cordero, Angel 103
Corrigan, Edward 47, 58, 60, 66–68
Cotton Exchange Stakes 45
Cottrell, James 107
Cottrell Stakes 35
Cottrill, William 56
Coulter, E. Merton 39
Cox, Albert 98
"Crescendo" John 81
Croker, Richard 78
Cumberland Stakes 54
Curator 75–76
Curule 109
Czar Nicholas 93

Dance Floor 107
Davis, Arthur 30
Davis, Charles Belmont 13, 15
Day, Pat 4
Day Star 26–27
Diomed 35
Distillers and Brewers' Stakes 45
Dixie Handicap 23, 48
Doble, Budd 22
The Dragon 82
Driscoll 88–89
Drummers Stakes 35
Duke of Montrose 45
Dwyer, Michael 34, 35, 45, 58, 78, 84, 98
Dwyer, Philip 34, 35, 45, 78
Dwyer Stakes 78

Index

Earl of Derby 3
Early 92
Eastin and Larrabie Farm 74
Ellison, Ralph 101
Emancipation Proclamation 11
Emperor of Norfolk 60
English Jockey Club 3
Eniskillen 44
Enlister 14
Epsom Derby viii, 3, 12, 29, 35, 55
Essex Stakes 66
Ewalt, Joseph 20

Falsetto 30, 54
Faugh-a-Ballagh 12
Favor 39–41
Feast of the Assumption 2
Ferdinand 51
Ferguson, Jim 63
Firenzi 61
First Mate 83
First Special 78, 84
First Sweepstakes 58
Fishburn 57
Flash Stakes 71
Flatbush Stakes 78
Fleetwood Stables 59
Fleischmann Stables 72
Florizar 87
Flying Ebony 99
Fonso 30–32, 39, 54, 83
Frank Fehr City Brewery Purse 49
Free Handicap 45
Freedmen's Bureau 77
French Jockey Club 3
Frister, Robert 101
Fusaichi Pegasus 109
Futurity Stakes 98

Gaines, Edison 107
Gallant Fox 99
Gas Company Stakes 58
Gazelle Stakes 98
General Pike 47
Gibbs, Charles 20
Gibson v. Mississippi 73
Glenbrook 97
Glidelia Stakes 57
Goodnight 47
Gordy, Berry 107
Governor Gray 101

Great Depression 45
Great Western Handicap 45, 49, 71
Greene, Henry 107
Gregory, Dick 110
Grey Eagle 6

Haggin, James Ben Ali 57–58, 61, 98
Haggins, Bud 97
Halma 74–76
Hamilton, Anthony 55, 98–99
Hand d'Or 85
Harper, Frank 22
Harry Gilmore 35–36
Hart Wallace 63
Hartack, William 94
Hawk-Eye 6
Hayes, Thomas P. 99–100
Hearst, George 98
Hemingway, Ernest 94
Henderson, Erskine "Babe" 7, 34–35,
  38–43, 45, 47
Henry, William 11, 16, 39
Henry of Navarre 78
High Tariff 63
Highflyer 36
Hill Gail 99
Himyar 25–27
Hindoo 35
Hindoo Stakes 57
His Eminence 88–89
Holloway, Cyrus 13
Honig, D. A. 66
Hotaling, Edward 5, 13, 18, 81–82
Hough, Williston 2
Hurd, "Babe" 7, 33–37, 39
Huron 66–69
Hyde Park Stakes 49

Ibsen, Henrik 20
Inventor 90–92
Irish Chief 67
Irish Pat 40
Iroquois 12
Isaac Murphy 57–58
Isabey 85

Jackson, Andrew 4–5
Jackson, John H. 98
Jacobin 48
Jerome, Leonard 47
Jerome Stakes 18

Index

Jesse 81
Jim Gore 48
Jockey Club 104–5
Joe Cotton 38–42, 57–58
Jordan, Eli 52
Jordan, Michael 53
Judge Himes 92
Juvenile Stakes 78

Kearney Stakes 45
Keene, Foxhall 98
Keene, James R. 98
Keeneland Library viii, 7, 15, 22, 52, 62, 67, 73, 88, 100
Kelly, Elisha Warfield 79–81
Kenner Stakes 23, 48, 55
Kentucky Alliance Against Racial and Political Repression 109
Kentucky Derby Museum vii
Kentucky Horse Park 65
Kentucky Oaks 48, 70–71, 99, 107
Keokuk 40
Kimball 30–32, 54
King, Henry 101
King, Martin Luther, III 110
King Alfonso 30, 39
King Clover 107
Kingfisher 84
Kingman 63–64
Ku Klux Klan 77
Kunze, Ed 64

Labold Brothers Stable 45
Lady Greenfield 52
Lady Violet 78
Lafitte 48
Lakeland, William 12–13, 30–32, 34–36, 54–55, 98
Lamplighter 78
Landsberg, William 98
Latonia Cup 48
Latonia Derby 99
Latonia Oaks 48, 71, 99
Laureate 75
Laurence Realization 78, 98
Law, Robin 4, 15
Layson 66
Leach, George B. 11, 14, 27
Leamington 12
Leamingtonian 100
Lee, Jimmy 48, 99–100

Leggett, William 103
Leonard 21, 54
Leonatus 100
Letcher, W. R. 60
Lewis, George Garrett 28–32, 54
Lewis, Isaac 44–49, 55
Lewis, Oliver 9–18, 39–40, 49, 97
Lexington 12, 35, 39
Lexington Ball 109
Lieber Karl 84–85, 89
Lieutenant Gibson 87
Lite Light 107
The Little Bighorn 19
Little Fred 97
Loftin 56
Logan, Hugh 3
Long, George J. 66–67
Longridge Farm 37
Lookout 64, 70
Lord Coleridge 40
Lord Murphy 54
Lorillard, Pierre 12, 98
Lost Cause 34, 36
Louisville Jockey Club 3, 16, 18, 21–23, 34–35, 41–42, 67
Lucky Debonair 51
Lyne, Lucien 66

Madden, John E. 23, 84, 89, 93
Maisons-Laffitte 93–94
Man o' War 65
Man o' War Memorial Park 65
Martin, Henry "Skeets" 80
Martin, Jack 66
Martin, Willie 75–76
McCarron, Chris 109
McClelland, Byron 44, 47, 74
McCreery 14
McDaniel, Hattie 96
McDowell, Thomas Clay 26, 90
McGrath, H. Price 10–18, 21, 38–40, 44
McGrathiana 11–12, 15–16, 44–45
Meridian 101
Merry Eyes 72
Metropolitan Handicap 98
Mint Jubilee 109
Miss Hawkins 70
Modjeska, Dame Helena 20
Mollie McCarthy 22–23
"Monkey" Simon 4–6

Index

Monmouth Handicap 61–62
Montgomery Stakes 35
Montrose 45–49
Moore, T. W. 90
Morgan, G. W. 100
Morris, John H. 67, 69
Morris and Patton Stable 39–40
Morrissey Stakes 45
Murphy, Green 53
Murphy, Isaac vii, 7, 21, 23, 30–32, 46, 48, 50–65, 67–68, 72–74, 76, 83, 92, 98–99
Murphy, Lucy Osborn 55, 64

Nichols, T. J. 26
Northern Wolf 107

Oaktown Stables 107
O'Connor, Flannery 1
Once Again 60
Ornament 70–71
Overton, "Monk" 23, 48, 63–64, 67–70, 74–76, 82, 99–100
Owings, Richard 51–52
Owings and Williams Stable 52, 54

Palii 1
Parmer, Charles 67, 105
Partez 107
Pat Malloy 34–35, 39, 45
Patti 45
Pendennis 46, 48
Perkins, James "Soup" 7, 70, 72–76, 82–83, 99–100
Perkins, William 76
Perret, Craig 109
Perry, Alex 42
Phil Dwyer 66–69
Phoenix Hotel Stakes 30, 57, 74
Planet 101
Plaudit 84–85, 89
Pleasant Green Hill Farm 51
Plessy v. Ferguson 82
Plutus 70
Pompei 81
Porter, William 98
Powhattan III 56
Preakness 71, 86
Prince Lubormoriski 93
Prioress 80
Promenade 78

Queen Mary 6
Quito 31

Ram's Horn 66
Randolph, John 81–82
Reconstruction 77
Redding, J. Saunders 30
Reiff, Johnny 80
Reiff, Lester 80
Renau, Lynn S. 14–16, 29, 42, 55, 80, 100, 105
Revoke 57
Revolutionary War 81
Riley 60
Ringgold, L. B. 82
The Rival 90–92
Robert Bruce 35–36
Runnymede 34–37
Russian Revolution 93

St. Julien, Marlon 108–9
St. Leger Stakes 45, 54
St. Louis Derby 23, 48, 71, 76, 98
St. Louis Fair Oaks 58
Salvator 62
Salvator Club 62
Sande, Earl 99
Sannazarro 89
Santa Anita Stable 46
Saratoga Cup 49
Sardonic 71
Sarong 12
Schmitt, Karl 106–8
Schorr, John W. 88–89
Scipio 81
Scott, Marvin 50
Scott, William 78
Scully, W. O. 25
Searcher 100
Second Special 78, 84
Semper Ego 82–83
Sharpton, The Reverend Al 110
Shauer, Charles 54
Shawhan, J. S. 30
Shoemaker, Willie 51
Simms, Willie 23, 77–86, 99–100
Sir Barton 65
Sir Hercules 12
Sitting Bull 19
slavery 4–6, 11, 15–16, 19, 26, 29–30, 33–34, 38, 42, 51, 81–82, 84, 96, 101–2

Sloan, Tod 79–80, 82
Sly Fox 86
Smith, Charles 87
Smith, George 55
Spinaway Stakes 48, 78
Stoops, William 97
Stoval, John 47–49, 99
Suburban Handicap 71, 84
Swift Stakes 78
Swigert, Dan 19
Swim, Robert 18–19, 21, 54

Tanner, David 51
Tarlton, L. P. 59
Ten Booker 40–42, 47, 57
Ten Broeck 22–23
Ten Broeck, Richard 80–81
Tennessee Derby 39, 70
Tennessee Oaks 48, 71, 76
Thistle 40
Thomas, Barak G. 25–27
Thraves, W. V. 37
Thrive 87
Tidal Stakes 78, 84
Tom Bowling 16
Tower, Whitney 102
Travers Stakes 69, 99
Traverser 71
Tremont Stakes 84
Triple Crown 65, 71, 86
Tupto 64
Turf Writers Association 95
Turner, Henry 77
Turner, Nash 90–92
Twyman, Winkfield 103
Typhoon II 70

Ulysses 82
United States Hotel Stakes 48, 55, 71
University of Louisville vii

Vagabond 14
Vagrant 19
Valenzuela, P. A. 103
Valera 70

Van Dusen, Clyde 87–88
Van Loan, Charles E. 9–10, 63, 105–8
Van Meter, F. B. 88
Vera Cruz 21, 30, 54
Verdigris 14, 17
Viley Stakes 30
Volante 58
Volcano 14, 17

Wagner 6
Wagner, Samuel C. 98
Walker, William 19–24, 54–55, 82–83, 98
Wallace, William 23, 82
Warrenton 97
Washington, Booker T. 33–34
Weatherwitch 30
Welch, Stephen 6
West, Ed 40–41
Whirlaway 51, 99
White 25
White, Raymond 107
Whitney, Eli 16
Williams, Carl 108
Williams, Howard 14, 17
Williams, J. T. 21, 39, 56
Williams, Jean 27, 31
Williams, Robert 82
Williams, "Tiny" 90–92, 99
Williamson, Ansel 15–16, 83–84
Winkfield, James 7, 55, 87–99, 102, 105
Winkfield, Robert 94
Winn, Matt J. 10, 18, 22–23, 35, 74, 82
The Winner 23, 82–83, 98
Withers Stakes 18, 84
Woodburn Stud Farm 30, 38–39
Woolley, Robert 38, 44–45
World War II 94

Young, Milton 34, 36, 42, 44–45, 47, 54, 60

Zev 99

www.ingramcontent.com/pod-product-compliance
Ingram Content Group UK Ltd.
Pitfield, Milton Keynes, MK11 3LW, UK
UKHW042017140426
5217IPUK00015B/1222

www.ingramcontent.com/pod-product-compliance
Ingram Content Group UK Ltd.
Pitfield, Milton Keynes, MK11 3LW, UK
UKHW042017140426
5217IPUK00015B/1222